God's DNA

God's DNA

A Metaphor For
The Holy Spirit's Ministry

Donald A. Broadwater

Scripture taken from the HOLY BIBLE, NEW INTERNATIONAL VERSION ®. Copyright © 1973, 1978, 1984 by International Bible Society. Used by permission of Zondervan. All rights reserved.

I used the Spirit of the Reformation Study Bible, Zondervan Publishing. Some of the verses quoted have emphasis added by this book's author.

"Twelve Strands of God's DNA" and "Spiritual Life Paradigm" are created by author, D.A. Broadwater.

All photography in the book is also that of the author.

This book was printed in the United States of America.

To order additional copies of this book, contact:
Xlibris Corporation
1-888-795-4274
www.Xlibris.com
Orders@Xlibris.com

42574

God's DNA

D-Dynamic N-Nucleus A-Activity!

"John answered them all, 'I baptize you with water. But one more powerful than I will come, the thongs of whose sandals I am not worthy to untie. He will baptize you with the Holy Spirit and with fire."
(Luke 3:16)

"He anointed us, set his seal of ownership on us, and put his Spirit in our hearts as a deposit, guaranteeing what is to come."
(2nd Corinthians 1:21)

"And we, who with unveiled faces all reflect the Lord's glory, are being transformed into his likeness, with ever-increasing glory, which comes from the Lord, who is the Spirit."
(2nd Corinthians 3:18)

"Therefore, if anyone is in Christ, he is a new creation: the old has gone, the new has come!"
(2nd Corinthians 5:17)

Dedication of this Book

To Gloria, my dear wife, who has always believed in me and encouraged me to write . . .

To Shirene our daughter, Chad our son, and Tanya our daughter in law, whose love has encouraged us from here to Australia!

And to our Grandchildren, Lorien, Elijah, and Kael, whose affections we hold so dear!

But most of all this is dedicated to the Lord of Life.

His Spirit keeps us on the journey while giving us so many friends to share their lives along the trail!

Appreciation

Gloria, Shirene and Chad were invaluable to me in this creative process.

I want to thank Dr. Judy Shoemaker for her editing expertise and her husband Jesse for giving us the gift of their friendship and time.

I also greatly benefited from Dr. Richard Pratt's insights to help me in completing this book. He continues to be a life friend.

Gloria and I remain inspired by our family and friends because we experience God's life in them as we journey in Jesus together.

Preface

I have heard over the years that you need to write about what you are passionate about. I have been a pastor for over 30 years and served in both Australia and America. And having returned to the States after 13 years overseas, I have been struck by what have been common characteristics to widely divergent ministries on both sides of the Pacific Ocean.

It has also struck me that these characteristics have shined through whatever the particular denominational clothing they were dressed in. Likewise, the size of a congregation also had relatively little impact upon them. It did matter in the sense that you simply couldn't do certain things unless you had enough people to do them. But this limitation did not change the basic premise that God had given *Life* to each ministry and that these *Life characteristics* were the same in every ministry no matter how diverse or distinctive these ministries might appear.

There were different emphasizes in various denominations to be sure, but not different *Life!* And the reason is simple: *God's Life* manifests itself with a certain *DNA (Dynamic Nucleus Activity)* no matter how different the personality or giftedness of the individual Body. And this got me to thinking about how believers would view themselves and their own churches if they really understood how much *Life* we share together because of Jesus pouring out of *His Spirit* upon the church. I have chosen to use *DNA* as a *metaphor* because

I believe it captures an important concept of describing the mystery of life that we share in Christ.

My wife and I have recently become friends with Will and Linda Bardon. They are retired from the Navy where they served for over 20 years in the medical field. Will has returned to medicine and now serves as a Physician's Assistant in our area. He shared with me some things from his knowledge of medicine that will give perspective for this study . . .

"DNA, which stands for deoxyribonucleic acid, is found inside the center or nucleus of a cell and contains instructions for the development of the cell. DNA is frequently described as a chain where the sections interlock in unique ways to create the cellular information. Those sections are called genes. Genes, either alone or in combination, will determine what features a person inherits. Scientists have been studying DNA for years and have found the more we learn, the more questions we have yet to answer."[1]

While my study defines the *DNA metaphor* as the *Dynamic Nucleus Activity* of *the Holy Spirit's ministry in us*, I pray that this will be helpful for the reader to consider just how powerfully *God's Life* is really alive in us to bring about the same "instructions for the development of the cell" in any expression of the Body of Christ.

Certain things, eternal things, remain true under all conditions and workings of the Holy Spirit. His signature can be seen wherever God is at work. We see this in the Book of the Acts of the Apostles as God's genetic code for ministry is manifested in the outpouring of the Spirit at Pentecost. As surely as you can see another human being is a human being because there are simply "human," and their DNA would confirm that; so surely is the signature of God's DNA in his

---

[1]   Will Bardon, Physician Assistant, Winter Haven, Florida, email of June 18, 2007, quoting WEB MD on DNA

people because when Christ poured out the Holy Spirit upon the church he poured his DNA into us!

Christ's Life has literally come to be *the Life* in the church. And *Christ's Life* comes to be the *Spirit Life Paradigm* for the church as the Holy Spirit brings *Christ's Life* to us. May the Spirit be gracious and manifest his *life* more and more in me . . . and in you . . . on a journey in Jesus . . .

Introduction

God's DNA: Spirit Life Paradigm

There have been all kinds of explanations suggested for what happened at Pentecost. When God first poured out his Spirit's Life upon the church it became obvious that God was at work. Many explanations of what happened at Pentecost have reduced this spiritual phenomenon to *a list* of things we *ought to be doing*. What this approach to ministry forgets is that Pentecost was not about what we need to be doing. It is about what God was doing and *what God continues to do by bringing Christ to dwell within God's people.*

Pentecost show us that you can't reduce the *mystery of life in the Spirit* to a *ministry model* that can be duplicated whenever we want. If it could wouldn't that have happened by now in America? May I ask you to consider whether any ministry program has brought lasting revival to this nation? What I believe we have seen is the hope for revival being shared; and we are very passionate about that. But our passion or our programs will not produce life in us or in others. Only God can do that!

What we need is a fundamental transformation of our lives and ministries. Only the Spirit of God can cause a person to be born again (John 3:5-7). Only the Spirit of God can enable a walk with Jesus (Galatians 3:1-3). And only the Spirit of God can bring about the awakening and revival that this nation needs (Acts 4:31).

Pentecost teaches us that it is not about having the right model for ministry. If anyone had a model for ministry that could not be improved upon it was Israel. God told Moses to make their ministry after the "pattern" he had seen on the Mountain as he met with God (Exodus 25:9, 40). And while this ministry was to be preformed it had no power to transform the lives of those believers who faithfully sought to maintain its ritual because their hearts could not be changed by the outward observance of any law (Hebrews 7:19). The author of the Epistle to the Hebrews puts it this way, "This is why Moses was warned when he was about to build the tabernacle: 'See to it that you make everything according to the pattern shown you on the mountain'" (Hebrews 8:5).

"But God found fault with the people and said, 'The time is coming, declares the Lord, when I will make a new covenant with the house of Israel and with the house of Judah. It will not be like the covenant I made with their fathers when I took them by the hand to lead them out of Egypt, because they did not remain faithful to my covenant, and I turned away from them. This is the covenant I will make with the house of Israel after that time, declares the Lord. I will put my laws in their minds and write them upon their hearts. I will be their God, and they will be my people. No longer will a man teach his neighbor, or a man his brother, saying, 'Know the Lord,' because they will all know me, from the least of them to the greatest. For I will forgive their wickedness and will remember their sins no more.' By calling this covenant 'new,' he has made the first one obsolete; and what is obsolete and aging will soon disappear" (Hebrews 8:8-13).

So it is not about getting our model for ministry right because if it was Israel would never have any problems! God gave a complete model for their ministry and they still went against him time and time again. The author of Hebrews points out that there was a reason for this and it rest with the people.

Even though God took them by the hand to lead them, it did nothing to change their hearts. As soon as God let go of their hand they would run away from him as quickly as little kids in a shopping mall do to their parents.

The only thing that changes this is if the hearts of those involved are changed. God did this by making a new covenant with his people though the death of his Son. Jesus paid the penalty for our sins so that our hearts could be forever connected to God and so that we might be enabled to now walk in his love. Then it didn't matter whether we felt God holding our hands all the time because we knew he had our hearts. His Spirit brought us awareness of his presence and we were moved to desire his will for our lives (Ezekiel 36:26-28).

Instruction manuals or programs for ministry can never create what only the Spirit of God can do as he connects our hearts to our heavenly Father's hand. When this happens we begin to walk with him and in the process of enjoying his presence we come to value what God alone can do in our lives. We seek his favor more and more as his Spirit moves us to desire new ways of living in obedience in response to his living presence in us.

The book of Acts shows us what happened as people's hearts were changed by the Spirit of God. Luke had already written the gospel named after him and he refers to this as "my former book" when he starts his preface in Acts (Acts 1:1). He says that the gospel of Luke recorded, "all that Jesus began to do and to teach until the day he was taken up to heaven." He then wrote Acts which recorded what Jesus continued to do and teach, except now it is through the agency of the church as empowered by his Holy Spirit.

Luke's record is a diary of what happened as God's presence returned to earth with the outpouring of the Holy Spirit upon the church. Jesus was on the throne in glory but he did not remain separate from the church's journey on earth. He poured out his Spirit upon the church so that he would continue to be with them to the end of the age. The church would never be perfect but she would be empowered and transformed by God's Spirit to be His witness to the world.

This would happen as *God's Life* was seen in *his people's lives* and inevitably as it was to be seen in *church Life*. Not in the activities of the church, but in the actual *Life of God* in the church. And this same process of God pouring out *his Life* into the church is *continuing* to happen. "In him the whole building is joined together and rises to become a holy temple in the Lord. And in him *you too* are being built together to become *a dwelling* in which *God lives by his Spirit*" (Ephesians 2:21-22, emphasis mine).

This is one of the most basic and awesome truths of Scripture. It declares that God has come to dwell among us again. Except this time not in our Savior's sandaled feet, but in his Spirit's presence as our sandaled feet shuffle, stumble, and fall; as they are strengthened, steadied, and enabled to walk, even run again.

It is a story about *God's Life* becoming our life. And because it is a story about what *God's life* is doing in us, it primarily is a story that remains forever about him. Paul says, "For we do not preach ourselves but Christ Jesus as Lord" (2nd Corinthians 4:5). We do this because it is Jesus who is still among us.

Whatever *life* is happening in the church comes as a direct result of *God's Life* being manifested in her. What Jesus promised he has fulfilled. In speaking of the outpouring of his Spirit upon the church, Jesus said, "*He lives* with you and will be *in you*. I will not leave you as orphans *I will come to you* . . . Because *I live, you will also live* . . . And on that day you will realize that I am in my Father, and you are in me, and *I am in you*" (John 14:17-20, emphasis mine).

This mystery of Christ being in us can never be simply reduced to a ministry model; a replication of things seen in the New Testament that were typical for the life of the church.

Things like "teaching" and "fellowship" are important. But participating in these things doesn't mean that you have Christ's Life alive in you; you may be simply walking through the order of service as a religious activity.

I remember visiting a church a number of years ago when a lady in front of my wife and me made the comment about the bulletin, "Well, what's on the menu today?" Now it is always cool when you can visit a church as a pastor and no one know that you are there. You hear some really honest comments and this lady was completely transparent about her view that going through a "worship service" was like going through a menu at a restaurant. My point being that you can go through a service and not experience Christ's life. You need for Jesus to come into your life for that to happen and when he comes his Spirit brings Christ's life to you. Christ's life brings us life. He is our life.

So if you want a model for ministry it has to be with God's Life at the center of it; the Holy Spirit bringing the life of Christ to us to be in us and with us forever! And this is a work of God not a model of men. That's why models for ministry cannot simply "transfer" ministry because any spiritual ministry is a ministry of the Spirit and if you want his ministry you have to go to him to get it! And when God comes he produces the "Spirit Life" after the pattern of his DNA for the church.

But we also can't help but notice that sin has also been at work to counter God's work. As the Spirit brought Life, time and time again, sin was at work to bring death. Satan tempted Adam in the Garden and Adam's disobedience brought death into the world (Genesis 3:1-6; Romans 5:12). And since that moment, every time someone sins death is brought into the world because death is always a consequence of sin (Romans 6:23).

That's why Paul speaks of Jesus' victory over them as being so much more abundant because his one act of obedience was greater than all of our disobedience. "For if, by the trespass of the one man, death reigned through that one man, how much more will those who receive *God's abundant provision of grace* and the *gift* of righteousness *reign in life* through the one man Jesus Christ" (emphasis mine, Romans 5:17).

The Bible declares that no matter how great the conflict between our sin and the consequences of them verses the work of the *Spirit to bring life* to God's people, *God's Spirit* will always overcomes sin's work of death because *God's work of Life* in believers may be hindered but it cannot be stopped. And we have proof of this because after the death of Jesus, we have the resurrection of Jesus. Paul tells us that this is a *"vindication by the Spirit"* (Romans 1:4) because God would not allow his *Son's Life* to end in the grave.

The Book of Acts is another Genesis story, a story of new beginnings. It is the genesis of *the Spirit-Life* alive in the church despite all that sin might do to destroy that *Life*. The church has much sin in her, but she has more *Life* in her. She has *the Spirit of Christ* at work in her, bringing *the Life of Christ* to her, transforming her, enabling her to overcome, not allowing sin to have the final word. And it is this *witness* that brings the greatest expression of the reality that Christ has been raised from the dead and is now exalted at the right hand of God in heaven!

The Bible is the Story of God's Life overcoming Death!

It is helpful to see this pattern throughout Scripture. The *Spirit* has always been at work. Since the beginning, *God's Spirit* was hovering over creation bringing about God's purposes here on earth (Genesis 1:2). When Adam sinned against God (Genesis 3:6), men's hearts became corrupt (Romans 5:12) and they turned more and more away from God (Romans 3:11-12) in pursuit of their own desires. This did not take long because Adam's first son murdered his second born (Genesis 4:8). All that God had done in creating the world and pronouncing it "good" was being threatened by a world corrupted by sin (Genesis 1:4, 10, 18, 21, 25; Romans 8:22).

God would not allow man's rebellion to win or *the Spirit's work* to be forever hindered. During the days of Noah God said, "*My Spirit* will not contend with man forever" (Genesis 6:3). God sent the flood that wiped man from the earth.

Grace was shown to Noah and his family (Genesis 6:8) and they were rescued on the ark that Noah had built under God's direction (Genesis 6:14-16). All of this showed *the Spirit's ministry* to warn people of their need for a walk with God; a walk that could alone be experienced by the same grace that Noah had known. This dramatically showed how life without the Spirit would bring death because when the Spirit stopped "contending" with man . . . men died!

Noah served as the example that a man would walk in grace and know the *life of the Spirit* despite all the corruption in the world around him. We too are called to that grace walk. The sin in our world is no excuse to say that God's Spirit is not able to give us the kind of life God wants us to live. He worked in Noah and we are called to see how he can work in us (Genesis 6:9; 2nd Peter 2:5-6; 1 John 1:7; 2:6).

The Spirit's Life gifts believers to overcome!

The Spirit's ministry doesn't just restrain sin as he did in the days of Noah. He also moves to gift men to advance God's kingdom purpose. We see this as Moses led the Israelites out of Egypt. As God was instructing Moses on how they were to live and worship, God told Moses that he would give the Israelites whatever gifts and skills necessary so they could fulfill their calling.

We see this as *the Spirit* called out a servant by the name of Bezalel. He was chosen and gifted to guide in the production of the tabernacle designs that God had given to Moses. "Then the Lord said to Moses, 'See, I have chosen Bezalel son of Uri, the son of Hur, of the tribe of Judah, and I have filled him with *the Spirit of God*, with skill, ability, and knowledge in all kinds of crafts-to make artistic designs for work in gold, silver and bronze, to cut and set stones, to work in wood, and to engage in all kinds of craftsmanship" (Exodus 31:1-5, emphasis mine).

The Spirit of God also "came upon" leaders so they could assist Moses in the leadership of Israel (Numbers 11:17). "Then the Lord came down in the cloud and spoke with him, and he took of the Spirit that was on him and put the Spirit on the seventy elders" (Numbers 11:25). At Mount Sinai, God came down in a cloud to meet with his people and proclaim his rule over them (Exodus 19:16-20:21).

We see similar events happening during Jesus' ministry. At Jesus' baptism, the Holy Spirit descended in the form of a dove while the Father spoke and said, "This is my Son, whom I love; with him I am well pleased" (Matthew 3:16-17). Later Jesus would take Peter, James and John with him up a high mountain on which he was transfigured before them (Matthew 17:1-2). Out of a cloud, God the Father spoke and said, "This is my Son, whom I love; with him I am well pleased. Listen to him" (Matthew 17:5). It is obvious that Jesus' ministry was confirmed by the Spirit coming upon him at his baptism and by God's voice calling us to listen to him.

At Pentecost Jesus ascended into heaven in a cloud (Acts 1:9) to be enthroned in heaven (Acts 2:30) and to forever establish his kingdom rule (Acts 2:35; 1st Corinthians 15:25). The Father gave Jesus the promised Holy Spirit to accomplish this through his outpouring of the Spirit upon the church (Acts 2:33).

This was an anointing of his people (1 John 2:20), an empowering of them (Luke 24:49; Acts 2:1-4), and a confirming of them as God's sons and daughters (Ephesians 1:14; Romans 8:15-17; Hebrews 2:11-12). It was the act of the Sovereign King of heaven and earth and so overwhelming that nothing less than our worship is adequate, nothing less than our service is due (Matthew 28:18-20).

Because God has now come down again through the presence of the Spirit, we know the presence of Jesus in our lives (John 14:17-18). We are enabled to live freely as God's children (John 8:35-36) but we are also empowered to witness as ambassadors of his kingdom rule (Acts 1:8; 2:35).

The cross brought Jesus agony on earth but led to his victory on the throne in heaven. This will one day bring about the complete victory of seeing Christ's rule here on earth as his kingdom is expanded until all his enemies are defeated (Acts 2:35). We are to pray for that kingdom to come here on earth as it is in heaven (Matthew 6:10). But in so doing we are not to forget that this kingdom has already come to us as believers. Jesus reminded us of this when he said, "Nor will people say, 'Here it is,' or 'There it is,' because the kingdom of God is within you" (Luke 17:21). God's Spirit has come to us bringing the kingdom rule of Jesus into our hearts and lives.

This same Spirit has now not only empowered us with Christ's presence but he has also gifted us with Christ's gifts so that we now have the ability to fulfill God's purpose for our lives as sons and daughters of the King of heaven (John 14:18; Ephesians 4:7). The Old Testament tabernacle and ministry were shadows of the new reality that we now have in Christ (Hebrews 8:5; 10:1). Only now, at Pentecost, the Spirit has been given without measure, in fullness, and upon all of God's people! And because of this we can now be used of God so that our witness to the community becomes a powerful proclamation of the presence and rule of Jesus.

This helps explain that what *the Spirit* was doing at Pentecost. He was bringing in fullness what he had already been demonstrating by example through the Old Testament. God's purposes for his people would be accomplished. But they would only be accomplished as *the people of God* were empowered by *the presence of God* for *the work of God.*

Salvation is always God's work. But because it is a work of God, it requires God to work! And where *God* is at work *God's life* is seen. It is powerful and it bears witness to the community that Christ lives! Not in just what is seen and the activity that results. But in *the Life* itself!

God's Life is seen in the DNA of the Holy Spirit's presence in the church!

We are going to be considering 12 characteristics of the *Holy Spirit's DNA* that can be seen in *the Life* that Jesus poured out upon the church. I have intentionally tried to avoid language that would give any particular congregation or denomination some sort of platform for thinking "theirs" was "the one" in view. Every denomination tends to have its own models for ministry and I don't want to be restricted in using the model of ministry language of our day. Instead I want us to look at the *Spirit Life* in Acts.

When we consider what actually happened as Christ poured out the Holy Spirit upon the church, and the life that this immediately brought, I don't know why we would ever want to get a cheap substitute for the kind of awesome things that happen when the Spirit starts to move in our midst. What we instead need to do is to seek him who alone can do the work that needs to be done by bringing God's life to us. What we need to do is to ask him to do what he always does when he comes!

We will be considering what I have called the *"Spirit Life Paradigm."* This is not intended to be another model for ministry that should be reproduced in the hope that life will come to a church. Only God brings life. There is no model for ministry that can produce spiritual life.

There are some models that are better than others because they more actually reflect what is found in the Bible. But as I have already said, without *Christ's Life* at work in us, models for ministry remain only that . . . models. I don't believe we need another model. There are already lots of those.

When I was growing up I used to love making model airplanes. But I don't ever remember ever being able to fly one of my "models!" The details in those planes can be incredible but you still end up with a plastic pilot sitting in a plastic cockpit. No amount of following the tedious directions that came with them can ever change that reality. And no matter how cool they look sitting on your shelf they will not fly. They have a plastic pilot and a plastic jet engine! He may have a smile on his face but he's going nowhere!

We don't need a model of something God may do. We need God to do something that only he can do. We need Jesus! And we need him to be sitting in the cockpit of our lives and flying us on the wings of his Spirit.

When Jesus breathes *His Life* into a church . . . that *church starts to live, really live!* Jesus said, "I am the Way, the Truth, and *the Life*" (John 14:6, emphasis mine). And it becomes obvious when *the Spirit* has brought *God's DNA* into his church because his *Life in us* becomes obvious. God starts changing us and teaching us how to fly!

Yet so many churches don't seem to be experiencing this in their church life. Could it be because too many churches are living out of their own perspective and their own desires instead of being yielded to the *Spirit's life ministry* among them? Isn't it worth considering that we may be hoping in the wrong things to work for us? Is it possible that we may have men bringing their programs for ministry to us, but we have never sought the Spirit's presence to bring his ministry among us?

I remember hearing the story about a lady who said she didn't like the new minister in her church. She didn't want anything to change in "her church" either. She made that very clear when she said, "I was here before this pastor came and I will be here after he's gone!" Wow! What an encouragement those words would have been to that new minister!

There wasn't much room for changes in her mind, let alone any kind of transformational life! From a human point of view, in a few short years, that type of attitude in any congregation will assure its' death. No new believer would feel comfortable very long in that type of ministry. And the reason is because *God's life* in them would be constantly going up against this attitude of death. And I can assure you, that *God's life* would win out. Either God would bring *revival* to that ministry by *the new life* he was bringing there through new people he was bringing or he would move those new people out because there was constant resistance to their *new life in Christ!*

You see God calls us to grow in *the life* we have *in Christ*. "Life newborn babies, crave pure spiritual milk, so that by it you may grow up in your salvation, now that you have tasted that the Lord is good" (1ˢᵗ Peter 2:2-3). He places a hunger in us as believers to want to grow in our *new life in Christ* and if that keeps getting resistance in ministries that don't want to change, God will burden his people to move to a ministry were they can grow.

We were meant as believers to know and grow in our *new life* in Christ. And it is *the Spirit of God* in us that literally moves us to know this. Now that we have tasted and seen what it is to experience the goodness of God in our lives, we will never be satisfied in a ministry that isn't encouraging *our life in Christ*. God's Spirit will assure that his people are feed spiritually so that they can grow in their *new life* together with others who want to grow.

How tragic it is for any ministry to have people with the attitude that they would rather die than change! God's life demands change. And without change we aren't experiencing God's life. There is a caution here. I remember hearing of C. S. Lewis saying about his church that he could take any change but only one per year!

So we have to be careful here. It's not change for change sake that I am speaking of but it is the changes that *God's*

Spirit brings to *God's people* that I am speaking of and these always bring *God's life*. One way or another *God's life* will win out! But what about churches that seems to be spiritually dead? Are they without hope?

Ezekiel had a vision showing why dead churches need the Spirit's Life!

Ezekiel spoke of this when he looked upon a valley of dry bones that were symbolic of what had become of the people of God in his day. God asked him, "Son of man, can these bones live?" And he replied, "O Sovereign Lord, you alone know" (Ezekiel 37:3).

Then God spoke to him and said that he should prophesy to those bones, that he should declare God's will over them foretelling what would one day be true, "I will make breath enter you, and you will come to life. I will attach tendons to you and make flesh come upon you and cover you with skin; I will put breath in you, and you will come to life. Then you will know that I am the Lord" (Ezekiel 37:4-6).

At Pentecost, *God breathed Life* into the dry bones of his people and they came to *Life!* Luke has recorded for us this spiritually-genetic moment. God had taken those who were spiritually dead (Ephesians 2:1-3) and made them *spiritually alive* in Christ (Ephesians 2:4-10)!

We can look at the *DNA (Dynamic Nucleus Activity)* of *God's Spirit* at work in the early church and see what the *Genesis of Life* looks like so that we might "turn to the Lord," asking him to complete his *Spirit's* work in us. He is still offering us this *Life*. But we must go to him to receive it!

God used Luke to record the Pentecost event for us. From this we have a written pattern of what his *Life* looks like as we see what happened as the result of *Christ* pouring our *his Spirit* upon the church. As we see what happened there on that day, it ought to cause us to cry out to God and ask him to do such a work in us. When we see what a movement of the *Spirit* looks likes, how can we settle for facsimiles or cheap manufactured reproductions?

If we understand how desperately we need *God's life* for this to happen, as we see that we cannot duplicate his *DNA*, we will again be forced to seek Jesus to come and *breathe his life* into our dead bones. Nothing less than his presence will do. Jesus alone can cause us to live. But he has promised, *"I am the resurrection and the life. He who believes in me will live"* (John 11:25, emphasis mine).

Consider this Overview:

1. God *breathed* into Adam and he became *a living being* (Genesis 2:7; 1st Corinthians 15:45).

2. When Adam sinned (Genesis 3:6-7) he died (Romans 5:12) *first spiritually* because he was now separated from God and later *physically* as his body returned to the dust (Genesis 3:19).

3. Ezekiel prophesied about a valley of dry bones that they would one day live as *the Spirit of God breathed life* into them again (Exodus 37:1-14).

4. Jesus *breathed* upon his disciples (John 20:22) and said to them, *"Receive the Holy Spirit,"* in anticipation of *the outpouring of his Spirit* upon his church (Acts 1:8; 2:17) that would guarantee their transformation and ministry.

5. Paul says that the *Holy Spirit* applies the finished work of Jesus to believers as he raises them from being spiritually dead so that they can live a *new life* now (Ephesians 1:18-20; 2:1-4; Romans 6:4; Titus 3:3-8) and will one day raise them from being physically dead as they are forever *transformed* into *the likeness of Jesus*

(1st Corinthians 15:42-52; 2nd Corinthians 3:16-18; 1st Thessalonians 4:13-18).

6. This happens as *the Holy Spirit* brings about *a complete transformation* of believers by *a process* that spans their entire life from their *regeneration* to their *glorification* (John 3:7; 14:17-20; 16:14; Romans 8:28-30).

7. *The Spirit* uses the *word of God* as the agent of transformation as he re-writes our *spiritual genetic code* (Hebrews 4:12; 8:10-12; 2nd Timothy 3:16-17) from being corrupted by sin as a *dna* (dysfunctional nucleus activity) *of the flesh* as we walked with the world (Genesis 2:17; 3:6; Romans 3:23; 6:23; Ephesians 2:1-3) into being a *DNA* (Dynamic Nucleus Activity) *of the Holy Spirit* reflecting a walk with Jesus (Deuteronomy 32:47; Ezekiel 36:27; John 17:17; Ephesians 2:4-10; 1 John 2:6; 3:9).

This begins at a spiritual cellular level in us as individuals but it will eventually completely transform what God is doing in the Body of Christ as a whole. Paul says, "The body is a unit, though it is made up of many parts and through all its parts are many, they form one body. So it is with Christ. For we were all baptized by one Spirit into one body-whether Jews or Greeks, slave or free-and we were all given the one Spirit to drink" (1st Corinthians 12:12-13).

What an awesome thing to consider that *God's Spirit* has literally brought *God's life* to us. It is wonderful to know that no matter how different we may be as individuals, we are all an important part of the Body of Christ. And how great to know that *the Life* we share in Jesus is a *Life* that reflects his Spirit now dwelling within us as members of Christ's Body. Paul says, "In him the whole building is joined together and rises to become a holy temple in the Lord. And in him you too are being built together to become a dwelling in which God lives by his Spirit" (Ephesians 2:21-22).

God's Spirit is dwelling in *God's people* writing *God's DNA* in our lives! His signature is evident. We will be considering 12 strands of this genetic code in this book. Each of these strands reflect the *Spirit's Life* in the Body of Christ and because of this, anyone who experiences them tastes something of *the life of God* being at work in the church.

It is for this reason that I believe that they evidence where God is working in his church and become opportunities for people who want to know more of God to be encouraged on that journey.

12 Strands in the Genetic Code of the Spirit's DNA of Ministry:[2]

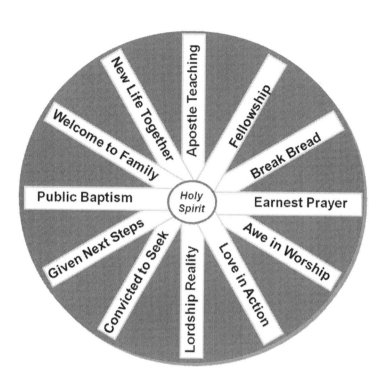

[2]   Donald A. Broadwater's Twelve Strands of God's DNA

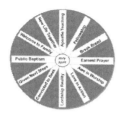

Chapter 1
God's DNA: Lordship Reality

No matter where you begin on a journey in Jesus if you don't end up at the point of realizing that Jesus is Lord, you haven't come to really know him, because he is Lord and if you know him, you know that.

Paul said to the church at Corinth that this was a key way in knowing if God's Spirit had really been at work in them. "Therefore I tell you that no one who is speaking by the Spirit of God says, 'Jesus be cursed,' and no one can say, 'Jesus is Lord,' except by the Holy Spirit" (1st Corinthians 12:3). Declaring the Lordship of Christ is fundamental to saving faith in him.

Paul told the believers at Rome the same thing. "That if you confess with your mouth, 'Jesus is Lord,' and believe in your heart that God raised him from the dead, you will be saved" (Romans 10:9). So failure to make such a confession obviously says that you are not a Christian yet.

The problem I see in evangelism today is that we try and get people to say these things without realizing what they really mean. When the Jewish audience heard Peter say that they had crucified Jesus, but God had raised him up from the dead, and seated him on the throne of David in heaven, it struck such terror in their heart that they cried out, "What must we do to be saved?"

This is critical if we are going to understand why so many responded to Peter's message. They were confronted with their complicity in the crucifixation of Jesus, "and you, with the help of wicked men, put him to death by nailing him to the cross" (Acts 2:23). But Peter didn't stop there. He told them that what they had done had actually been part of, "God's set purpose" (Acts 2:23). They had done what they had done willingly, but unknowingly being part of a plan that God was orchestrating for the redemption of his people. This meant that they were being shown to be desperately and completely out of control and without hope unless God showed them mercy. They had been participants in making sure that Jesus was nailed, but they hadn't realized that their actions had also nailed them! They had thought that they were in control and stopping Jesus once and for all. But Peter now tells them that they weren't in control at all and unless they are shown mercy they had no hope!

God had raised the very Jesus they had crucified! God had freed him from the agony of death, "because it was impossible for death to keep its hold on him" (Acts 2:24). They had killed Jesus, but it was impossible for their actions to succeed in keeping him dead. He is the Lord of Life!

David had died and anyone listening to Peter could have visited his tomb (Acts 2:29). But if you visited the tomb of Jesus, you would find it empty! He had been raised from the dead! He had ascended into heaven and taken his rightful place to rule from his throne in glory (Acts 2:30).

And if that were not enough *to show them* how they had partnered in committing the worse sin in the universe, Peter said that what they were now seeing demonstrated before their very eyes was the outpouring of the Spirit that Joel had prophesied!

God was now witnessing against them from the heavens! He was witnessing to fact that Jesus had been raised from the dead. He was witnessing to the fact that his kingdom could not be stopped. He was witnessing to the fact that Jesus was in control of that kingdom as King. And he was witnessing to the fact that they now stood before the God of the universe as condemned men. All of this was being witnessed to by the outpouring of God's Spirit upon his people who had become witnesses of this themselves!

Over three thousand heard this message. They repented and turned their lives over to Christ! They devoted themselves to learn more from the apostles and you could find them meeting in each others' homes taking their meals together. They even shared their financial wealth to make sure that none among them was in need! You can read about this in Acts 2:36-47.

Why aren't people responding to Christ today like this?

In today's evangelism we forget that most people just don't have the Scriptural background to understand any of these things and so it is little wonder that they do not feel the deep need for repentance because they do not realize that their sin has offended the God of the universe. They just think that they may have messed up a little, but no big deal! And so if they do "believe in Jesus," it is often a sort of sentimentality that remembers the babe in the manger story. They are really sorry about him growing up and having to suffer so much. They are glad that he was raised from the dead. But they really have no idea just who this Jesus is as Lord of the universe! And so they have no real understanding as to why they really do need his mercy or the power of his Spirit to be at work in them!

Many people no longer believe that God really created the heavens and the earth. They think that random events of time and chance and some primeval slim evolved into this awesome universe. People no longer believe that the Bible is the inspired Word of God. They think it is just one version of some naïve people's view of religion. People no longer believe that their sin has personally offended the God of the universe. So they really aren't worried about anything they have done because any psychologist can tell them, "It's your mothers fault!" Or, if it wasn't your mother's fault, "It was the fault of those you grew up with!" But one thing you never hear any more is, "It's your fault! Deal with it! Go to God for help and mercy and deliverance from it!"

You see most people just don't believe any of the basic truths of the Scripture any more. They don't even know them because they are preached or taught in churches like they were a generation ago. So how can people come to understand what it means that, "God has made this Jesus, whom you crucified, both Lord and Christ!" unless we explain a lot more to them than we are presently doing?

Peter sets the stage for true evangelism by showing us the way. He lets us know by his message and example how important it is to explain to people exactly what it is that they have done to be culpable for their own personal sins. He lets us know by his preaching that it is really important to explain to people in the context of their own lives and culture, just exactly how this Jesus is now The One in their universe that they should be concerned about having offended! Peter lets us know that we have to explain just who Jesus is and why Jesus came and what position Jesus now holds as Lord of the universe for people to understand that unless they are reconciled to him they shall forever be lost!

And we need to do the same thing!

The Jews in Peter's day were able to pick up on what was happening because they knew about Joel's prophecy about the outpouring of the Spirit, and so when Peter said that what they were now witnessing was the result of the crucified/raised/ascended/enthroned Jesus now at work, they knew they were in trouble!

There had been a Coronation of the King in heaven and they were now witnessing the ordination of his servants on earth. They were being anointed to extend his kingdom rule.

They had been given his Spirit so that they would be enabled to spread the message of his kingdom with the authority and power of the King. And they were told not to stop until he had returned!

The Jews who were hearing this message knew that their only hope would be if the King of the universe should show them mercy. He had no reason to be merciful to them because they had put him to death on a tree! But they were being told by Peter that the offer for their forgiveness, a royal pardon, was being extended to them by the King himself.

Why wouldn't anyone want to accept that offer?

It is this *DNA* characteristic of the Holy Spirit's ministry in making the *"Lordship Reality"* known to people that we must ask God for once again. If this first *DNA* characteristic is not restored to the heart of our message there will be no one seeking the Lord of Life because they will not understand that they are already standing in the gates of death. Instead men will at best just seek to take out a fire insurance policy with Jesus.

Christianity isn't a fire insurance policy against judgment

But Christianity isn't a sort of "eternal policy" that has no impact in your life today. If you get Jesus you get life now! It will not only take care of you when you die, but you will start being transformed by Christ's life now.

But when people think that they have "accepted Jesus" under the terms of *"an eternal fire insurance policy"* (protecting against the fire of judgment), they have misunderstood that you can't have *life* then and not have *life* now! It is called *eternal life* for a reason. It comes to a believer now and continues for eternity.

And in the interim, Christ's life begins to transform every part of our life because when you get Christ you get his Lordship over you. It's not a matter of keeping up with the "policy payments" by attending church once in a while and throwing something in the collection plate when it is passed. It's not a matter of having a commitment card in your back pocket. It's a matter of having the life of God in your heart now!

Some people say that they came to Christ during a crisis in their life. And sometimes people are genuinely converted at these times because they realize their desperate condition. They may have gotten cancer. Or their spouse may be in the hospital dying from an infection. Or a child may have been struck by a car. They may have lost their job and are about to lose their home. It could be one of many crisis situations that cause people to think of their need of God.

But unless that person has had the Spirit of God working in their life, when the crisis is over, so is their "faith." There is even a bit of a joke about people who "get religion" only to forget where they put it later! The way you know that you have experienced real faith is because it is real later, after the crisis has past. You must ask, "Are you continuing to follow Jesus after the immediate reason for your first seeking him has gone?"

Some may have even had their first experience of Jesus while attending a church service. You may have come along quite innocently but to your surprise actually found Christians enjoying themselves in worship! This may have challenged your life and you may have longed to discover that kind of joy for yourself. But it doesn't come from just singing their songs! It comes from God's calling you to an eternal relationship with Jesus so that He becomes your song.

Christianity isn't for a season but for an eternity!

Christianity is about a living relationship with the Living God and you don't come to that on your own or just take it up when you decide it might be good for your life. Paul says you come to know this as the Spirit of God is at work in your life bringing you to a place of acknowledging, "Jesus is Lord." This implies an awareness of what it means that Jesus is Lord and what it means for you to be yielding your life to his Lordship over you.

How can this be real for you?

At some point, no matter what originally started your interest in the gospel, no matter why you felt drawn to pursue a journey in Jesus, you must come to realize, as Peter said, that, "God has made this Jesus, whom you crucified, both Lord and Christ" (Acts 2:36).

We become aware of our sin and ask God's forgiveness for it. We may not have been there when they crucified our Lord but we come to realize that our reaction to what happened to him would have been no different than theirs.

We may have been among the disciples who denied him or we may have participated by being among the crowd who demanded, "Crucify him!" (Matthew 26:69-74; 27:22). But we would have been there doing the same things they did. Our sins have made all of us culpable in his death. As Paul said, "We all sinned and fall short of the glory of God" (Romans 3:23).

Yet as hard as it is for us to admit that we are sinners, it is not enough if we stop there. We must also come to understand that the only provision we have to take care of the debt that we owe is one that God himself must give us. Psalm 49:7-8 says, "No man can redeem the life of another or give to God a ransom for him-the ransom for a life is costly, no payment is ever enough."

But what man could not do, God did for man through the giving of his only Son. Jesus knew this was his calling and he willingly yielded his life to the plan of God. "For even the Son of Man did not come to be served, but to serve, and to give his life as a ransom for many" (Mark 10:45).

And now that the ransom has been made, the forgiveness of any who call upon him is assured. "If we confess our sins, he is faithful and just and will forgive us our sins and purify us from all unrighteousness. But if anybody does sin, we have one who speaks to the Father in our defense-Jesus Christ, the Righteous One. He is the atoning sacrifice for our sins, and not only for ours but also for the sins of the whole world" (1 John 1:9; 2:1-2).

How can a person ever know if this has happened for them? How can a person know that they really are forgiven and that there is no longer any condemnation being held against them in heaven? Heaven is a long way from us and we have no physical way of seeing if our names are in the Lamb's book of life (Revelation 20:15). So how can we be sure that we belong to God?

Growing up I remember hearing Paul Harvey say on his radio program, "And now for the rest of the story." The rest of the story is, "And this is how we know that he lives in us: We know it by the Spirit he gave us" (1 John 3:24). The message of Acts declares that the Spirit has come (Acts 2:34). God is calling people to himself through faith in God's Son and he is empowering them to be his witnesses (Acts 2:17). "And you will receive the gift of the Holy Spirit. The promise is for you and your children and for all who are far off-for all whom the Lord our God will call" (Acts 2:39).

Christ is on the Throne and ruling over all men!

Whether men think about it or not, every morning that they arise to start a new day, everything that happens during that day, every thought that they have, every word that they speak, every attitude they express, is all coming under the searching eyes of Him with Whom we will have to do!

Christ has been raised victoriously from the dead! He has proven that He is the Son of God and rightful heir of the Throne of God by His resurrection (Romans 1:3-4). And He now sits in glory on that Throne until all His enemies are defeated (Acts 2:35).

He is in absolute control of the universe and is bringing all things in the universe under his headship and rule. This means trouble to all those who remain enemies of God, but it also means blessings will come to those who through faith have come to know Christ and yield themselves to his Lordship!

There is no place that you can go to escape his rule; no country, no city, no cave where his rule does not extend. In the last book of the Bible, Revelation, there is a description of the terror of men before the presence of Christ when He comes. "Then the kings of the earth, the princes, the generals, the rich, the mighty, and every slave and every free man hid in caves and among the rocks of the mountains. They called to the mountains and the rocks, 'Fall on us and hide us from the face of Him who sits on the throne and from the wrath of the Lamb! For the great day of their wrath has come, and who can stand?'" (Revelation 6:15-17)

Christ's rule will either threaten your plans or fulfill them!

The reality of Christ's Lordship doesn't always strike fear. It should if you are opposed to him or the advancement of his kingdom (Psalm 2). But if you know him and are yielded to his purposes for your life, his rule actually guarantees their fulfillment! Psalm 138:8 says, "The LORD will fulfill *his purpose* for me; your love, O LORD, endures forever—do not abandon the works of your hands."

God intends that his rule actually comfort us. David said, "Before a word is on my tongue you know it completely, O Lord. Where can I go from your Spirit? Where can I flee from your presence? If I go up to the heavens, you are there; if I make my bed in the depths, you are there. If I rise on the wings of the dawn, if I settle on the far side of the sea, even there your hand will guide me, your right hand will hold me fast" (Psalm 139:4, 7-10).

Comfort for the believer but terror for those who have rejected Christ's Lordship: This is *"the Lordship Reality"* whether men want to acknowledge him or not. And this is one of the *DNA* characteristics of God's Spirit being at work; to remind men of this *"Lordship Reality"* and call men to faith in God's Son to escape the coming wrath.

The Holy Spirit extends the rule of Christ

This is the simple truth: *Christ is Lord* of the universe and this *Lordship Reality* is the controlling factor over everything that now happens in the universe. "And God placed all things under His feet and appointed Him to be head over everything for the church, which is his body, the fullness of him who fills everything in every way" (Ephesians 1:22).

Jesus said that when he sent his Spirit the reality of Christ's rule would be impressed upon the hearts and lives of everyman. "When he comes, he will convict the world of guilt in regard to sin and righteousness and judgment: in regard to sin, because men do not believe me; in regard to righteousness, because I am going to the Father, where you can see me no longer; and in regard to judgment, because of the prince of this world now stands condemned" (John 16:8-11).

King David knew what it was to see God's rule extended over men

David knew it what it was to have the rule of God on his side. He had seen firsthand what would happen if nations and kings tried to fight against the living God or his eternal purpose. He penned these words to remind us of the *Lordship Reality* that all men will face, "Why do the nations conspire and the peoples plot in vain? The kings of the earth take their stand and the rulers gather together against the Lord and against his Anointed One, 'Let us break their chains,' they say, 'and throw off their fetters.' The One enthroned in heaven laughs; the Lord scoffs at them. Then he rebukes them in his anger and terrifies them in his wrath, saying, 'I have installed my King on Zion, my holy hill'" (Psalm 2:1-6).

Paul says God also rules in behalf of believers

Paul says something similar to the church of the Thessalonians. He tells them that Jesus is going to come back and repay all those who have opposed them or done them harm! And the reason was because Christ is now ruling over their hearts and lives so anyone who opposes them is now directly opposing the Lord of glory and will pay for it!

"God is just: He will pay back trouble to those who trouble you and give relief to you who are troubled, and to us as well. This will happen when the Lord Jesus is revealed from heaven in blazing fire with his powerful angels. He will punish those who do not know God and do not obey the gospel of our Lord Jesus. They will be punished with everlasting destruction and shut out from the presence of the Lord and from the majesty of his power on the day he comes to be glorified in his holy people and to be marveled at among all those who have believed. This includes you, because you believed our testimony to you!" (2nd Thessalonians 1:6-10)

You and I are now part of Christ continuing to extend His kingdom!

And this includes you too if you have believed in Jesus as your Lord! God is coming to be glorified in you and will deal with those who have insulted his work of grace in your life by opposing his rule over you! Wow!

While working on this chapter I got a phone call from the air conditioning repair man. Our house is on the market to sell and we are having an open house tomorrow. We had our carpets cleaned yesterday and everything was going along great until I noticed that the air conditioner wasn't working!

It is 90 degrees in our Florida home. Mother lives with us and she is almost 80. And we have an open house to show how everything in our house is perfect! Do you get the picture on how grateful I was to just get the call from the air conditioning firm to let me know he was 15 minutes from the house and on his way?

How much more should we be excited that Jesus is on his way! Are things a mess in our lives? Yes. Are there things that are broken in our lives? You bet. But Jesus is our Lord! And he has paid the complete price for all that it will take to deal with anything in our life or deal with anyone who is hindering our life with him! Nothing is going to stop that! No flat tire on the "repair truck" or failed "repair policy" from heaven! The deal is sealed! And it has been sealed with his blood and delivered to us by his Spirit's work in our lives.

Pentecost declares that God's Kingdom continues to come!

Christ will return one day to finalize his rule over men and finally defeat all his enemies, handing over the completed kingdom to the Father (1st Corinthians 15:24-28). But this rule is being extended right now! And he is extending his rule through the power of the Holy Spirit attesting by what Jesus is continuing to do since, "Jesus is Lord."

Pentecost is the sign that God's kingdom purpose will be fulfilled, not just in us, but in the church as a whole, and in the universe! Jesus has poured out His Spirit to bring about his kingdom in us so that others might see their need of him and cry out, "What must we do to be saved?"

It's not just a matter of getting forgiven. It's a matter of coming to be a son or daughter of the Most High God, the King of kings, and Lord of lords with all the privileges and responsibilities that flow from that! No wonder we need the Holy Spirit in our lives to anoint us, seal us, and empower our lives; to comfort us when we fail, and strengthen us once again so that we may keep in step with him.

No wonder Paul said, "Are you so foolish? After beginning with the Spirit, are you now trying to obtain your goal by human effort?" (Galatians 3:3) "Since we live by the Spirit, let us keep in step with the Spirit." (Galatians 5:25)

Think about it. If we would never have come to know God unless the Spirit of God brought us to faith in Christ, why would we be able to live for God apart from Him? We need his Spirit to enable us to walk with Jesus.

Consider how this Lordship Reality impacts your life:

1. Have you looked at the heavens lately? Read Psalm 19 and then go for a walk asking God to make His glory and His power known to you.

2. Did you know that God made all of His creation to not only reflect His glory, but to benefit you? Read Psalm 8.

3. Why is it, do you suppose, that with all the kind things that God does for us, we still resist His will and find ourselves even fighting against His ruling over us? Read Matthew 6:25-33; Romans 1:20-23; 3:23; 8:7-8.

4. What things are now present in your life which reflect an attitude or action that has been rejecting Christ's Lordship?

5. Does your rejecting His Lordship in this area of your life change Christ's status in heaven? Read Hebrews 1:8. Who does our rebellion effect? Read Hebrews 10:26-31.

6. Read Colossians 1:15-23

   a. Who created all things? (v. 16)

   b. Who is holding all things together? (v. 17)

   c. Who can hold you until you come before God? (v. 22)

7. Are you in the hands of Jesus? Why not stop right now and surrender your life under His Lordship if you have never made that commitment. And if you are a Christian, what area in your life do you need to trust him for his power and peace to overcome? Ask the Holy Spirit to work in you those things pleasing in his sight, and watch him work!

Chapter 2
God's DNA: Convicted to Seek

When the Lordship of Christ is proclaimed, people come under conviction of the sin that is in their lives and they start to feel their distance from God. The thing of it is God is moving in them to show them their need for Christ. And this comes because they are starting to hear just how exalted Christ really is.

It is hard to grasp why this truth is offensive to those who see themselves as evangelicals, but choices are being made about the kind of ministry that people want to have. And tragically many of those choices are being made in a way that intentionally keeps any deep truth of Scripture from being heard. More and more churches are choosing to keep people from hearing anything that is perceived to be "too heavy."

We want people to feel good about God. We want people to feel good about how they feel about themselves. And we want people to feel good about what they want to do with their lives.

When is it good to feel bad?

But feeling good about things does not mean that we are good. Just because we might feel right about something does not make it right before God. Only God can make us right. And when God is starting to make us right before him, we usually start to feel wrong because we begin to see ourselves as God see us: sinners who are in need of mercy. We start to see that we aren't good at all (Romans 3:12).

Unless this happens, unless we start to feel bad about our lives, we will never seek to be right before God. We will never see how far we are from God if we feel good about everything. In the Psalms David spoke of this when he said, "An oracle is within my heart concerning the sinfulness of the wicked; There is no fear of God before his eyes. For in his own eyes he flatters himself too much to detect or hate his sin" (Psalm 36:1-2).

When this is the case we see no need for mercy because we have done nothing that requires it. And in this expressed belief we show how far we are from God. Or to put it in David's terms, "the fear of God." It is little wonder why we see so few seeking God or his mercy. Men have been told by other men that they should feel good about themselves. They have not been told this by God. And unless we tell them what God's word says, they will persist in believing they must be right because they feel so good.

We need to feel bad about our lives. We need to see how wrong we have been about God and about where we stand with him. We need, in particular, to see that unless God makes us right we will never feel good about ourselves again.

We need to come under "conviction" for all the wrong we have done so that we will seek the only one who can make us right before God. We need to see our need of Jesus. He is God's solution for us being wrong, for us being sinners, for us being God's sworn enemy (Romans 5:8).

Jesus is the one who paid the debt for our sins to make us right before God. He is the only one who can reconcile us to God. "Salvation is found in no one else, for there is no other name under heaven given to men by which we must be saved" (Acts 3:12).

He saves us by actually paying the debt that we had acquired before the holy God. He does this by the shedding of his blood. This is the payment God required. "In fact, the law requires that nearly everything be cleansed with blood, and without the shedding of blood there is no forgiveness" (Hebrews 9:22). This is the payment Jesus made, "so Christ was sacrificed once to take away the sins of many people" (Hebrews 9:28).

And when we realize all that it cost him for us to be made right before God, we should really feel bad, but grateful and embrace Jesus as our Savior and Lord. Then we will have reason to feel good about ourselves and about our relationship with God because Jesus will have actually made us right in God's eyes through our faith in him. "God made him who had no sin to be sin for us, so that in him we might become the righteousness of God" (2nd Corinthians 5:21).

How bad have things gotten?

In both America and in Australia, even church leaders are now talking about how hard it is to speak of moral absolutes with their people. How is it that we have come so far that the 10 Commandments have become 10 Considerations? How is it that the simple truths of God's Word are no longer defining our lives and ministries?

Don't we realize that Jesus is Lord and that he hasn't changed? "Jesus Christ is the same yesterday, today and forever" (Hebrews 13:8). Don't we realize that Jesus said, "Light has come into the world, but men loved darkness instead of light because their deeds were evil," and we only facilitate that darkness by not confronting men with the light (John 3:19)?

Don't we know that men will continue to remain under the wrath of God unless they come to Jesus (John 3:18)? Don't we realize that they will never come to Jesus unless they get convicted of their sins and see their need of him? But that's not going to happen because we have now become uncomfortable about telling people the Bible teaches moral absolutes!

We need to again see the value of God's law! They are not social comments on life they are God's commandments for living! And Paul says that they when they are proclaimed they show us our need of Jesus. "So the law was put in charge to lead us to Christ that we might be justified by faith" (Galatians 3:24).

Is it right to call people who believe what is true "fanatics?"

Today's culture makes those who believe the Bible seen to be fanatical. But is it being fanatical to want to understand what is true in the universe? And what could be more reasonable than to want to know what the God who has made the universe and told us what is true? The only fanatical thing is the gospel which declares that the God of the universe, who has no reason to do anything other than hate us for what we have done to his universe and his Son, has loved us! And yet this is true. "For God so loved the world that he gave his one and only Son, that whoever believes in him shall not perish but have eternal life" (John 3:16).

The gospel proclaims the fanatical love of God!

When you look at Acts 2, and Peter's proclamation of what is now true because of Christ's exaltation to the right hand of God and his enthronement in glory, you see people coming under conviction about what is true. They realized that their direct involvement in, or their complicity with, or their indifference to the crucifixation of Christ, implicated them in His murderous death. Peter said, "Therefore let all Israel be assured of this: God has made this Jesus, whom you crucified, both Lord and Christ" (Acts 2:36)!

In the Old Testament, people were stoned at the testimony of two or three witnesses if evidence was given that they had broken God's law. "Anyone who rejected the Law of Moses died without mercy on the testimony of two or three witnesses" (Hebrews 10:28). And now Peter was standing to proclaim to the entire crowd that they had in fact been guilty of something far worse. They were guilty of crucifying the Son of God! The very One God had confirmed as his anointed by enthroning him in glory as both Lord and Christ, they had crucified!

The reality of Christ's Lordship brought terror to the souls of those who heard Peter's message. "When the people heard this, they were cut to the heart" (Acts 2:37).

In light of the reality of Christ's Lordship, people came under conviction of their sin. And may I say again, that this is one of the most missed elements in today's churches. We want people to come along and hear some great teaching, or experience fellowship; we want them to have a great time in worship and even know that if they have a need, our church will pray for them or help them out in any way that we can. But where are we seeing the need for "conviction" being central to our ministries? Where are the churches that see it to be a good thing that people are coming under conviction about sin in their lives?

To make up for the disastrous absence of this element of God' DNA, his Spirit's signature in the church that he is at work in the hearts and lives of people, we challenge them by saying, "You may know God as your Savior, but make him your Lord today."

How shallow this sounds next to the reality of Christ's Lordship which already exists over the universe and will one day be made known to all men (1st Corinthians 15:25; Philippians 2:10)! We don't make him anything! He is King of kings and Lord of lords and ours is but to acknowledge who Jesus already is and fall before him asking him for mercy and giving him worship in response to his grace to us (Revelation 17:14).

Fanatical love calls for fanatical commitment!

This is what Peter is calling for when people, having come under conviction, cry out, "What must we do?" and Peter replied, "Repent and be baptized, every one of you in the name of Jesus Christ!" (Acts 2:37-37) Their repentance (in the original language of the New Testament "repentance" means "a change of mind") would show that they were now thinking about their lives, their priorities, and their plans in light of Christ's Lordship over them. And their baptism would be the public witness that they had made this commitment.

I believe this fundamental element of *God's DNA*, this coming under sufficient conviction for sin so that relief is sought in Jesus, is a signature of his Spirit's presence and power and must again be sought through the proclamation of *Christ's Lordship*.

The absence of conviction is the result of men and women, boys and girls, not knowing that Jesus is the Lord of Glory and that their eternal destiny is in his hands and his hands alone. Through the proclamation of God's word, and through our personal witness to it, we must again show people why grace is needed. Only then will grace be sought and his favor experienced. But make no mistake about it, without this fundamental element of *God's DNA* present in the message of the church, we should expect few conversions.

And why should non-Christians on the outside of the church come under conviction when so many on the inside of the church have such a shallow understanding of their faith? Without *"conviction"* as part of the *DNA of the Spirit's work* in our ministry, we will have a spiritually deformed genetic code of ministry and life.

Is this being "negative?"

To say these things is not to be negative. It is in fact one of the most positive things that can be stated for the presence of conviction is a sign of spiritual life. Whether expressed for the first time by a person who has just started seeking God, or expressed by a mature believer, conviction is a positive ministry of the Holy Spirit. After David sinned with Bathsheba and came under conviction for that sin having been confronted by Nathan the prophet, he penned these words from Psalm 51:11-3.

"Have mercy on me, O God, according to your unfailing love; according to your great compassion blot out my transgressions. Wash away all my iniquity and cleanse me from my sin. For I know my transgressions, and my sin is always before me."

David could not go another moment in his life without getting right with God! Oh, that this glorious element of God's DNA would be restored to believers in God's churches! She would not only be purified from her sins, she would be empowered to witness.

David affirms this in Psalm 51 by saying, "Cleanse me with hyssop, and I will be clean; wash me and I will be whiter than snow. Let me hear joy and gladness; let the bones you have crushed rejoice. Hide your face from my sins, and blot out all my iniquity. Create in me a pure heart, O God, and renew a steadfast spirit within me. Do not cast me from your presence or take your Holy Spirit from me. Restore to me the joy of your salvation and grant me a willing spirit, to sustain me. Then I will teach transgressors your ways, and sinners will turn back to you" (Psalm 51:7-12).

There are several things that David says here that are critical to understand. First of all he longed for the cleansing that Christ accomplished for us through the shedding of his blood on the cross. He looked forward to that cleansing; we can now look back to it and claim it by faith as God's provision for the cleansing of our sins. "How much more, then, will the blood of Christ, who through the eternal Spirit offered himself unblemished to God, cleanse our consciences from acts that lead to death, so that we may serve the living God" (Hebrews 9:14).

Secondly, one of the reasons that David wanted God's forgiveness was because he didn't want the ministry of the Holy Spirit quenched in his life. He knew that his sin would separate him from having fellowship with God. He pleaded with God for cleansing because he didn't want the Spirit's presence to be taken from him. Again, how things would be different today if believers were that concerned about not hindering God's Spirit! The Holy Spirit would be powerfully at work in our individual lives as well as in the ministry life of our congregations!

And thirdly, note the impact that a "cleansed" believer has upon others. David says that if he is cleansed, if the Holy Spirit's ministry in his life is not marginalized or hindered by God's presence being taken from him, "Then I will teach transgressors your ways, and sinners will turn back to you" (Psalm 51:13).

You can't take people where you haven't gone. You can't tell other people that they need to leave their sin if you haven't left yours! You can't show people what a cleansed life looks like if they can't see it in you!

Have you ever thought about the fact that one of the reasons we aren't seeing more people coming to faith in Christ around us, around our churches and in our communities is because they can't see faith in Christ being lived out in us? They don't see us being troubled by our own sin. They don't see us expressing any conviction. We need to again see *conviction* as a good thing; as a key element in *the Spirit's DNA* for the church.

How long will this "conviction" DNA be effective in us?

Conviction is not something which will ever leave a Christian for believers should always feel compelled to flee to Christ whenever sin has crept into their lives; whether it came in around back or crashed in through the front door! And once a believer has been convicted about something, cleansed from it, and changed by the Holy Spirit's ministry though it, it becomes a conviction for life that keeps a believer from desiring to take that same road again.

Not everyone who has been convicted by Christ seeks him for forgiveness. Some hear the word of life and choose death. But others seek him and live. Both of these results are seen throughout the New Testament.

When Jesus spoke to the woman at the well, he spoke to her about her need for living water because of the long drink she had from the well of adultery (John 4:13,18). Jesus healed the lame man at the pool by showing him the power of His authority to simply say, "Get up! Pick up your mat and walk!" He later appeared to him warning, "Stop sinning or something worse may happen to you!" (John 5:8, 14) Both of these show people who became convicted, cleansed, and changed! We know for example that the converted woman at the well went home and reached her entire community through her changed life and witness for Christ (John 4:39-41).

But such was not always the case. Others who were convicted by his message also left from following him. Jesus said, "I am the bread of life. He who comes to me will never go hungry, and he who believes in me will never be thirsty." (John 6:35) But He also warned, "No one can come to me unless the Father who sent me draws him, and I will raise Him up at the last day." (John 6:44) And as a result, many of his disciples turned back and no longer followed him (John 6:66).

When the reality of his absolute Lordship is proclaimed, sin will be subsequently exposed. Some will come to believe in Him, others will leave from following Him any further. But choices will be made as people are convicted by His words.

It is good to be convicted about what is bad!

Paul says of the Thessalonians' response to the gospel, "For we know, brothers loved by God, that He has chosen you, because our gospel came to you not simply with words, but also with power, with the Holy Spirit and with deep conviction" (1st Thessalonians 1:4-5). The presence of the Holy Spirit brought, Paul says, "deep conviction."

And it was a sign, a signature of God's grace and calling upon them, God's DNA being stamped into their lives, because the Life of Christ was becoming evident through the lives of the Thessalonians. "And so you became a model to all the believers in Macedonia and Achaia. The Lord's message rang out from you not only in Macedonia and Achaia-your faith in God has become known everywhere!" (1st Thessalonians 1:7-8) When the gospel was preached and the Thessalonians started responding to the gospel, being under conviction and getting rid of their idols, Paul knew that God had chosen them and put his Spirit in their lives.

This sign of God's DNA was obvious in the church in Acts 2 as Peter preached about the Lordship of Christ. People were convicted of their sins, they were cut to the heart, and they cried out, "Brothers, what shall we do?"

May we hear that cry once again because of what the Spirit is doing in our lives as the people of God!

Consider whether you have been "Convicted to Seek"

1. Are you living under the Reality of Christ's Lordship?

    a. When Isaiah saw God on His Throne, and heard the angels crying out, "Holy, Holy, Holy is the Lord Almighty," did he come under conviction? Read Isaiah 6:1-5

    b. What about John the Apostle when he was brought into the presence of the resurrected Lord of Glory? Did his response show that he was afraid of being in His presence? Read: Revelation 1:17-18.

   c. What does Paul say ought to be the response
      of any seeker who comes to realize that God is
      present with His people?

      Read: 1st Corinthians 14:24-25

2. Have you had such an experience? Write it down if you
   have and reflect upon how it may have been painful for
   the moment, God was bringing your sin to your attention
   so that you might run from it to Christ who had died to
   be the payment for your sin.

3. Consider now, in private meditation, what needs to be
   cleansed from your life because as a believer you are
   to live in His presence because He is present in you:

   a. What do you need to release from your life? What
      burden have you carried for too long?

   b. What also needs to be forgiven in your life? What
      haven't we been honest to God about? What do
      you pray others will forgive you for?

        "If we claim to be without sin, we deceive
      ourselves and the truth is not in us. If we confess
      our sins, he is faithful and just and will forgive us
      our sins and purify us from all unrighteousness." (1
      John 1:8-9).

4. POINT: Don't fear being "convicted!" It is a ministry of
   God's Spirit in you!

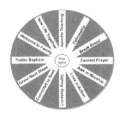

Chapter 3
God's DNA: Giving of Next Steps

When I was 19 years old I attended a community college for a semester in southwest Virginia. I wasn't a believer at that time and I certainly had no idea that I would one day go into the ministry. So I followed the first year course work for an entrée student and calculus was on the list.

I thought I was pretty good at math until I took that course. And as lost as I was spiritually, I became that lost in the world of math. One of the things that didn't help was that I didn't have any idea what I wanted to do so I was just passing time hoping something better would turn up.

But there was another thing that didn't help. I had a professor that had, what I have been told isn't all that unique, an interesting teaching style. He would walk into the room, pick up a piece of chalk, and write a formula the length of the black board. He would then turn and walk back out the door.

I didn't make it in that class. Over the years I have come to see that there are a lot of people who are seeking to know more about God but they aren't going to make it either, at least not in the average church. People are hurt by what they encounter in the "classroom of the church."

People in Ministry and Pendulums in Motion

As the pendulum swings, there are some ministries that never worry about what they see to be "too much theology." They never seem concerned about what people actually believe about the Bible or its relevance to their lives. They want to keep their faith simple.

Yet if you are honest about their ministries, they often do more than many churches who profess everyone's need to understand the deep theological truths of the Bible. These believers are often out there touching people's lives for Christ. They help people whenever they can; they are available; and they live as servants of others for Jesus' sake. The problem is they really do need to understand more of what God's Word says so that they can actually be more effective in doing what they love to do in ministering to people.

On the other side of the pendulum, there are ministries that struggle to help people connect the dots between what God says and how it applies to their lives. The reason seems to be that they don't know how to do it themselves. Their belief is that you just preach at people, teach them lots of good stuff from the Bible, heavy stuff, and eventually it will just work out in their lives. Their belief is that if the Bible is correctly taught it will be caught. There is no intentional discipling in this model, only the suggestion that it should be done.

A Journey in Jesus is truth lived in love along the trail . . .

Paul says, "So then, *just as you received* Christ Jesus as Lord, *continue to journey in him*" (Colossians 2:6, my translation and italics). This tells us that there are two fundamental sides of our walk with God. The first is in understanding what it means to come to know him as our Lord. The second is in our understanding that we are on a journey that must continually express his Lordship in practical-loving ways.

Jesus spoke of this when he said, "I am the way, the truth, and the life" (John 14:6). He is the way to truth on which we ought to be experiencing his life. This is more than just practical stuff done for others. And it is more than just being preachy. It is a life journey in Jesus.

If you look at how believers actually journeyed in Jesus in the New Testament, it is obvious that they made the connection between what Jesus had done for them on the cross and how they were to live in him. You can't look at what happened in Acts 2:42-47 with believers in the church and fail to see this kind of deep-practical life journey. God had loved them and they were showing the love of God to one another. It was just what Jesus had taught the disciples (John 13:34). And it was just what the apostles were teaching the church. Strong theology was being taught, but strong love was being shown.

They didn't just learn more from the apostles so that they could go around saying how much they were learning. They sat at the apostles' feet so that their own feet could get moving for God! There wasn't a distinction between what Jesus or his apostles taught and its application to their lives. There was harmony in these things. They learned from what the apostles taught them and having been changed by what they learned, they quickly moved to love and teach others.

Is Theology "taught" or "caught" or both?"

Theology isn't just taught it is lived or you don't have Biblical theology! God's word warns us that if we only have knowledge we become arrogant because we haven't been humbled by the love that is required to apply those truths in a broken world. Paul said, "Knowledge puffs up, but love builds up" (1st Corinthians 8:1). So if people are only learning and not loving, they haven't got the pendulum swing right yet. You may know that you need to serve others, but it takes humility to wash their feet so that they can understand the love of God in practical ways.

I often tell people, "Journey in truth but let love set the pace." We may want to get something across to people, and they may desperately need to hear it. But if we aren't showing them the love of God along the way and helping them take *the next step* they need to take on their own personal journey, anything we say will get lost in the shuffle of life.

Don't just tell them God loves them; wash some feet and show them that God loves them! Help people take *the next step* they need to take on their journey. They will not know how to "wash" another person's feet if you don't give them the example by washing theirs!

Pharisees embarrass people instead of encouraging them!

If people feel like their questions are going to be treated as stupid, you have not helped them on their journey at all. You have only given the reason to believe that they must journey alone. You have only succeeded in making another cynical believer who is afraid to open their heart to others.

That's one of the things that the Pharisees did well. They wanted everyone to know how smart they were about the Bible but they didn't want to take the time to actually help anyone. They just threw their rule book at people and told them they should know better.

Jesus told the people of his day that the Pharisees loved their positions of power. They loved to "sit at Moses seat" (Matthew 22:2). But Jesus warned people that the Pharisees, "do not practice what they preach." By this Jesus was saying that it is never enough to point out something if it is not lived out.

But they did more than fail to do things themselves. They put obligations of the law upon people that even they could not keep. "They tie up heavy loads and put them on men's shoulders, but they themselves are not willing to lift a finger to move them" (Matthew 23:4).

They knew a lot about the Bible, but they were unwilling to put themselves out there to help people. They wanted people's respect and submission, but they wouldn't "lift a finger" to help people in any practical way to do the very things they had told the people they must do to be spiritual!

Jesus warned us of what their outcome would be, "Woe to you experts in the law, because you have taken away the key to knowledge. You yourselves have not entered, and you have hindered those who are entering" (Luke 11:52).

Pharisees pretend they are experts and never enter in themselves!

One practical implication of this is to consider what kind of ministry you are having. Does your ministry consider itself to be an "expert" in its particular field of ministry? If so consider this: You may be spending so much time learning how to become an "expert" that you never actually take the time to enter into what you have learned by applying it in your life. Jesus warns us that one of the ways we will know that we are doing this is if we try and hinder others who want to actually "enter in." If we don't get it, we will try and hinder others who want to.

How tragic that this has become true in so many sections of church life. Believers are told that they should go to the next seminar, but haven't been encouraged to apply what they learned at the last seminar! What good is it to learn that you must love your husband or wife more if you don't actually do that? It could only be worse if those who attended the seminar actually became critical of those who were trying to apply what they had learned.

And that is happening. Today believers are being spiritually harassed by those who know much but who help little! If we demand standards of spirituality, and then fail in helping the very people we have demanded them from, we have become Pharisees!

Jesus' ministry always gave people practical "next steps"

When you contrast this with the ministry that Jesus brought the differences are obvious. He said, "Now that I, your Lord and Teacher, have washed your feet, you also should wash one another's feet. I have set you an example that you should do as I have done for you" (John 13:14-15).

Did you get that? Jesus is the 'Teacher' and he washed feet! He didn't just tell them that God loved them, "he showed them the full extent of his love," by taking off his outer garments to take up the towel and basin (John 13:1).

The church in Acts after the outpouring of the Spirit of God, demonstrates this same life of Jesus. People are shown the love of God in the most practical of ways. Next steps are sought, given, and taken. They gather in one another's homes and share their lives, their food, and their financial resources while they lift one another up in prayer and praise their God (Acts 2:42-47).

When the Spirit of God is at work, so is this *DNA* ministry of *"Giving Next Steps"* to help people on their journey in Jesus. People are shown how they might pursue their own journey with God. Journeys take place one step at a time! Ministry ought to be showing people what steps they need to take and them show them how to take them.

The ministry of the Spirit is one in which men are moved to help others in ways that they need to be ministered to. God doesn't just leave his sheep out to wander. He goes after them and guides them until they are safely home. And when Christ is alive in us through his Spirit we do the same things!

Giving of Next Steps have always been part of the Spirit's ministry

When people who were seeking to get right with God came to John the Baptist and asked him, "What should we do then?" John didn't say, "Go figure it out for yourself if you can." He didn't say, "Come back tomorrow for another lesson in "Repentance Theology 101."

No! When John preached he not only told them to, "Repent," he told them how. John answered, "The man with two tunics should share with him who has none, and the one who has food should do the same" (Luke 3:11). John gave them practical stuff to do in order that they make connection with the heavy theology they were hearing. He helped them know how to pursue a journey in Jesus; he didn't just tell them they had to have one!

The same thing happened when tax collectors asked what they were supposed to do. John gave them something practical they could do, he gave them steps they could follow, in order that their lives showed they were truly repentant. "Don't collect any more than you are required to." (Luke 3:13) And he did the same when soldiers asked. John told them, "Don't exhort money and don't accuse people falsely-be content with your pay." (Luke 3:14)

The point being that the New Testament is filled with examples of how people were given the next steps they could take to pursue a journey with Jesus. They were very practical things to express the heavy theology they were being taught. This is part of *God's DNA* for the church.

Practical ministry is Spiritual ministry!

Jesus says that it's the application of what is being taught that shows you have understood. "Therefore everyone who hears these words of mine and *puts them into practice* is like a wise man who built his house on the rock" (Matthew 7:24).

He showed how serious this was by saying, "Not everyone who says to me, 'Lord, Lord,' will enter the kingdom of heaven, but only he who does the will of my Father who is in heaven." (Matthew 7:21)

You can't say that you "get it" because you understand a lot of theology. Jesus says that if that's all you've got, you don't "get it" at all! You might appear smart before men, but He's not impressed because the only thing He is interested in is whether you are applying what you know. That's why the church that doesn't know a lot of theology but applies all they know is experiencing tremendous growth and blessing! And that's also why those who know a lot, and who tend to look down on those who don't, often aren't experiencing growth.

Houses get built as workers come to work and pick up their hammers, follow the blueprint, and start to pound nails!

Jesus said to the paralyzed man, pick up your mat; to the needy, don't worry about their lives; to the critical, stop judging your brothers; and to a dead man he said, "Lazarus, come out!" (John 11:43).

Incredible theology was being taught! How faith in God could overcome the crippling effects of unbelief; how trust in a loving Father in heaven would not be misplaced; how people who are critical will one day have heaven's mirror held up to their face and they will be found far more wanting than those they spent their lives being critical of; and how dead men can live because of the One who holds *Life* in his hands!

We have got to start teaching more theology in ministries where little exists because people will never come to know the depth of the love that God has for them if we don't. But we also have to get those who have arm-chair theologies into some street ministries!

Real theology is truth in practice. If you every doubt that look at Jesus! He is *the Living Word of God*. His life is not only the incarnation of God, but the incarnation of truth and the incarnation of love. He has come so that men might really live and help others to discover *the Life* that God wants them to have.

And when you look at Acts, you see the same thing happening. You see Peter declaring that Christ is Lord, and people crying out under conviction, "What must we do to be saved?" and then Peter telling them in a very practical way that they need to "Repent" and begin to show the evidence of that repentance by making a public profession of faith through baptism.

People were given very practical ways to pursue a relationship with God and express that with others. So people did not count their possessions as their own but sold their lands and properties as people came to be in need (Acts 2:45; 4:34). Believers also choose 7 men to serve as deacons because some widows were being overlooked in the food line (Acts 6:1-6). And Philip took the time to explain a passage of Scripture after running a bit of a marathon to catch up with an Ethiopian in a chariot who needed Christ (Acts 8: 30-38).

Spiritual ministry made easy!

It's not that hard, it really isn't. But we make it hard because we want to stay in our comfort zone of being in control. When God is at work, when his *DNA* is manifesting itself, his *Spirit* is moving to reach men for Christ. He is also enabling his people to provide practical ways to help people so that they will be *"Given their Next Steps"* in their journey in Jesus.

Ezekiel prophesied about the day coming when *God's Spirit* would move people to obey God. "And I will put my Spirit in you and move you to follow my decrees and be careful to keep my laws" (Ezekiel 36:27).

Let me ask you, "Is God moving in your life?" One way you know that he is moving in you is because you are taking *the next steps* you need to take with him. Paul says, "Since we live by the Spirit, let us keep in step with the Spirit" (Galatians 5:25).

Considerations on "Giving Next Steps" to others:

1. Some believers think that anything simple or practical isn't very spiritual.

   What does the Bible say about practical ministry?

   Read Matthew 10:42; James 1:27; 2:14-26; 1 John 3:17-18

2. Perhaps we have all had teachers who didn't help us at all in knowing how to take the next steps in our assignments.

   What can you do in your ministry to help make sure that those who are seeking God can know what steps they can next take to discover a deep journey with God? Read Ecclesiastes 4:9-12; Hebrews 10:19-25

3. What next steps have you been afraid to take? Why not ask the Holy Spirit to get you moving in that direction?

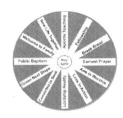

Chapter 4
God's DNA: Public Baptism

Perhaps one of the most overlooked characteristics in today's churches is *God's DNA of baptism*. Churches want to have wonderful worship experiences, they want to have the Bible taught, they want to have great fellowship with one another, they want to share their faith, and they even want to help care for one another in loving ways; but all of this should be shaped by this fundamental strain of *God's DNA*, his *Dynamic Nucleus Activity*, the outward sign of the inward work of his Holy Spirit's presence in his people's lives.

When people were giving their lives to God in response to the preaching of John the Baptist, they submitted themselves to public baptism. They were struck with *the reality of God's Lordship* and came under *conviction* for the way they had lived. They then asked John what *personal steps* they needed to take to have a life that reflected their faith with integrity. John told tax collectors to not collect more than they were supposed to collect; he told soldiers to not be harsh with authority by taking advantage of people by extorting money or threatening them with false arrest. To the average citizen, John said that they should share whatever they could with others. All were *given next steps* to take.

But in addition to the "personal" commitments they made in how they were to conduct their lives with one another, all of these reflected things that were relevant to them as individuals, their own way of life and their own pattern of sin, they were all given the same requirement for making a "public" commitment; they were all to be publicly *baptized*.

Baptism is the public witness to the personal work of the Spirit

Pentecost was the time the Israelites celebrated the first fruits of their annual harvest. God was gathering many into his kingdom family as the firstfruits of the harvest that would be reaped from the nations. And while the world was watching, the people who were turning to Jesus were being baptized.

They were publically showing their commitment to Jesus as their Messiah and King. Christ had been enthroned in glory and now believers were showing his enthronement in their hearts. The reality of Christ's forgiveness and Lordship over believers would be publically seen. What had been received privately in one's heart would now through baptism be acknowledged publically. God had forgiven and now that forgiveness would be celebrated with the Christian community and before the watching world challenging others to think about their need for Christ.

Baptism manifested God's DNA

Baptism reflected *the Spirit's DNA* ministry because it reflected the fact that their past had been washed away by the blood of Jesus. Nothing speaks more to life than this. "But when the kindness and love of God our Savior appeared, he saved us, not because of righteous things we had done, but because of his mercy. He saved us through the washing of rebirth and renewal by the Holy Spirit whom he poured out on us generously through Jesus Christ our Savior" (Titus 3:4-6).

Paul here reminds us that it was the outpouring of the Spirit that brought the cleansing blood of Jesus to be applied to our lives. And as a result of being cleansed, believers could now be filled with the power of God. They were now able to think about the direction of their lives and chose to take advantage of the new beginning God had given them. They had received new life from Christ and their lives would now be new.

When Peter said, "Repent and be baptized, every one of you, in the name of Jesus Christ for the forgiveness of your sins" (Acts 2:38) we see people responding to the gospel by repenting and being baptized. And we see their lives reflecting the forgiveness that God had promised to give them.

Baptism was present as the church was birthed at Pentecost because it is a fundamental strain of *God's DNA*. It is present as part of *the genetic code* of the church that had come to be alive with the *Life of Christ* in her. It was a public reflection of what was a personal reality; they had been spiritually *"baptized by the Spirit,"* and now they were being publically baptized in recognition of this.

Baptism put everyone on the same playing field

There is something else baptism does. It puts everyone on the same playing field. It prevents some from thinking they are making a more noble or spiritual commitment than someone else. No one was advantaged by money or disadvantaged by not having any. Baptism would not make people of higher social standing stand out from those who had no social standing. They were all standing together to be baptized.

This sign reminds us that before God there is no favoritism. If anyone was to be saved from their sins they needed the same remedy. They needed for their sins to be forgiven and Jesus' shed blood provided the only means by which that forgiveness could be obtained.

As the Spirit of God works without favoritism in whom God so desires, so the sign of baptism is placed uniformly upon those whom God has called. It doesn't matter what their nationality or personal histories or baggage. Part of *God's spiritual DNA* is giving of the same Spirit, his *Holy Spirit*, to everyone he calls. That's why physical *baptism* reflects this spiritual reality.

What other things does baptism represent?

Where sin had once isolated a person from God, baptism showed acceptance from Him. Where going one's own way was once the chief characteristic seen in a person, they were now submitting to the way of Christ. Where they had once been ashamed of Jesus and His words, they were now ready to own Him as their own Lord.

Where they had once been outsiders to the kingdom of God, they were now made to be recipients of it! Where they had once been separate from any of God's promises to His people, they were now made to be heirs of His covenant promises; promises that would also have implications for their children. Where they had formerly never started on a journey in Jesus, they were now publically setting out on one. Where they had never been a part of the family of God, baptism reflected their entrance into God's family and members of it along with countless numbers of brothers and sisters of all nations throughout all ages!

Baptism is about more than water!

So it wasn't just a little water on the head after all! It wasn't even about being immersed into it! It reflected a conversion from being in the kingdom of darkness to being in the kingdom of light. There is nothing more significant in a believer's life than this outward-physical expression of inward-spiritual grace.

So why we don't see it as part of the *DNA* for the church; why we don't see it as actually expressing *"Life"* within the Body; why we don't celebrate it more and challenge more to respond to the *Holy Spirit's movement* in their hearts to be baptized? And why haven't we seen its central significance in previous paradigms for *Life* within *the Body*? When we fail to see how important baptism actually is, we say something significant about the state of health within the Body; and it is not good.

Baptism is about changed lives!

My wife and I recently visited a large Baptist church in Orlando, Florida. On that particular Sunday, twenty people were baptized. What a blessing to be there and witness twenty people, of different ages, of different economic status, of different nations being baptized. It was like a breath of fresh air! *Life* in the *Church Body!*

Despite all the bad press the church is getting in our day, here was a place where people were routinely, through there is never anything routine about the *Spirit's work* in people's lives, making this public commitment. But as wonderful as this was, and it was, it really was, I thought about what it must have been like to see, "three thousand added to their number" on one day and another "two thousand" soon afterward (Acts 2:41; 4:4)!

Baptism is a sign of God's awesome work in the souls of men

Man, how awesome God is! What a day that would have been to have witnessed 3,000 brought to Jesus and baptized! How wonderful it would have been to be part of it! But if you don't get anything else know that the sheer numbers of people coming to Christ during those early church days was seen to only be the firstfruits of the great ingathering of God!

We have come to accept as *"normal"* almost no movement of God in our midst. But when *the Spirit comes* people are converted and baptisms are regularly seen. And why does this happen? Because it is the extension of the rule of Christ in the hearts of men, an extension that is guaranteed by his presence upon the throne from which he will continue to rule until all his enemies are either converted or conquered! "Therefore God exalted him to the highest place and gave him the name that is above every name, that at the name of Jesus every knee should bow and every tongue confess that Jesus Christ is Lord to the glory of God the Father" (Philippians 2:9-11).

There will be no stopping of the advancement of Christ's kingdom and his kingdom is advanced through the conquering of the souls of men as they repent and acknowledge their surrender to him as Lord of Life.

Paul told those gathered in Athens to hear his message, "In the past God overlooked such ignorance, but now he commands all people everywhere to repent" (Acts 17:30). This is the identical message Peter had preached at Pentecost. And why should anyone repent and turn to God? "For he has set a day when he will judge the world with justice by the man he has appointed. He has given proof of this to all men by raising him from the dead" (Acts 17:31).

What God is doing in conquering the hearts of men will be seen!

People hear the gospel and find out that despite all the powers of hell trying to prevent the redemption of God's people through the slaying of God's Son, that God actually used the wickedness of men to accomplish His purpose (Acts 2:23-24). They find out that Jesus has been exalted to the right hand of the Father in heaven and placed upon the Throne. They find out that he has received from the Father the promised Holy Spirit and has poured him out upon the church! And men find themselves being convicted of the way they have lived their lives and they are driven to seek what steps they need to take to express genuine repentance. *Baptism* is the outward sign that *the Spirit of grace* is at work in them. It shows part of the *Spirit's DNA* at work.

How dramatic that first day must have been when 3,000 souls were added to the church. What a baptism that would have been with everyone having the sign of God's cleansing in their lives!

Why are we divided over the sign God has given to show our unity?

We get angry at each other within the Christian Body about how much water was used! Did they immerse? Did they pour? Did they sprinkle? I imagine with 3,000 being baptized a little of everything happened!

I can imagine there being one gentleman who had eaten well all his life. As he was stepping into the river, his foot slipped on one of the rocks and he ended up going under and being *immersed* while his splash caused the water to be *poured* over the next guy! The guy beside him, still standing on the water's edge, caught some of the water as it splashed over the second guy causing him to be *sprinkled* with the baptismal mist! I can imagine that happening with 3,000 people coming to be baptized! Can you?

But what I can't imagine is any of them being worried about how they were baptized. I can only imagine them rejoicing that they were. We get side-tracked with the externals and so often and forget that the whole deal is really about the awesome thing *God is doing!*

Imagine the 3,000, whose complicity in Jesus' crucifixation Peter had publically exposed, that you were now seeing their faces released from guilt that had been heavy on their hearts. Imagine how grateful they would now be in knowing that Jesus' blood which had previously been the testimony of their guilt had now become the testimony of their innocence! Does anyone really think that they would have been worried about how much water was used?

Think also about how their public baptism was now putting them at jeopardy of being hunted down by the Roman government as followers of this insurrectionist Jesus! The Romans would have seen their extermination as the next phase of "Operation Wipe Out." They had crucified the ring leader. Now they were bound to turn on his followers. They could allow no other Caesar!

So believers were literally putting their lives at risk. They were actually receiving the "mark" of resistance by being publically baptized! Rome would not have simply overlooked another uprising, especially when 3,000 were involved in such a public demonstration against what would be seen to be Roman rule.

And when you are putting your life on the line in making such a statement of your faith and allegiance to King Jesus by being baptized, you aren't going to be thinking about whether you are being immersed, poured, or sprinkled! You know that your baptism has now sealed your public testimony for Christ and there is no turning back for you no matter how much water went over your body!

Baptism also speaks of what the Spirit will continue to do in your life!

These saints were crying out from their hearts, "Brethren what shall we do?" And they were told by Peter what to do, "Repent and be baptized!" They were seeking relief from their conviction and Peter told them the next step they should take to make this personal commitment to Jesus' Lordship a public reality. But he also told them that they wouldn't be making their journey alone because he added, "And you will receive the gift of the Holy Spirit" (Acts 2:38).

Later the apostle Paul would clarify that public baptism would point to the greater spiritual reality of *the Spirit's baptism* in every believer. "For we were all baptized by one Spirit into one body-whether Jews or Greeks, slave or free—and we were all given the one Spirit to drink" (1st Corinthians 12:13). Being physically baptized doesn't make you a Christian, but it does reflect the reality of the ministry of the Holy Spirit in all believers' lives.

And what the Holy Spirit has started he will continue to work out in our lives. Paul says that we have been "marked" in him, that we have received the "seal of the Holy Spirit" so that as God looks down from heaven upon us there is no doubt as to who his children are (Ephesians 1:13). And he goes on to say that the Holy Spirit is, "a deposit guaranteeing our inheritance until the redemption of those who are God's possession-to the praise of his glory" (Ephesians 1:14). God has called us, marked us, sealed us, and guaranteed our future inheritance as God's kids all because of the gift of the Holy Spirit being given to us (Acts 2:38).

Baptism also reminds us that it's not just about us, but others too!

Peter didn't miss the opportunity God had given him. The awesome thing that had just happened for the 3,000 was just the beginning of the ingathering! That's what the Old Testament celebration of Pentecost was all about. It celebrated the starting of the harvest in anticipation of what God would do during the actual harvest (Exodus 23:16; Numbers 28:26).

And the harvest of redemption flowing from Christ's finished work has started! Jesus had poured out his Spirit upon his church to get things going but he wasn't finished. He was only beginning!

Peter made this point when he said, "The promise is for you and your children and for all who are far off-for all whom the Lord our God will call" (Acts 2:39).

If I could paraphrase what is meant here, it might sound something like this, "Aren't there others you are concerned about too? Don't you all have loved ones and friends who need to hear this awesome message of forgiveness? And what about people you meet along your journey? Don't you think they would love to hear this message? Where could any of these people hear a message of grace such as the one you have come to believe in today? Don't leave anyone out! Go and tell whoever you can and see what God will do!"

You see the message of forgiveness that the 3,000 had heard and responded to wasn't just for them! God was going to call others to himself and they all needed to know that what the Holy Spirit had started to do there at Pentecost was just the beginning; a firstfruits of the harvest!

Baptism is a sign of God's covenant promises being extended to others

When Peter says, "The promise is for you and your children and for all who are far off-for all whom the Lord our God will call," he is unmistakably using covenantal language. God is saying through Peter that he hasn't changed his mind. In the Old Testament the covenant of God's promises extended to not only Abraham but to his seed after him. That's why God told Abraham to put the covenantal sign of circumcision upon Isaac (Genesis 17:1-14). And now Peter is saying to his newly converted Jewish brethren, that the covenantal promises are for their children as well and for anyone else whom God chooses to call.

There would have been no Jewish brother who would have missed this point. Isaiah had prophesied, "The Redeemer will come to Zion, to those in Jacob who repent of their sins,' declares the Lord. 'As for me, this is my covenant with them,' says the Lord. 'My Spirit, who is on you, and my words that I have put in your mouth will not depart from your mouth, or from the mouths of your children, or from the mouths of their descendants from this time on and forever,' says the Lord" (Isaiah 59:20-21).

Are we going to argue over the blessing of God's covenant promises?

How can God's DNA be an obstacle to the very fellowship it is genetically designed by God to produce? But we seem to have a propensity to make this happen in our arguments over how much water "must be used!" We even fight over whether to "baptize" or "dedicate" our kids to God!

Over the years I have intentionally worshiped at a host of different congregations with my wife. On the beautiful Gold Coast of Australia we have worshipped in Pentecostal churches as well as Baptist and Presbyterian churches.

I have taught seminars at church camps in Australia where brothers across denominational lines have come to hear God's word. And here in the States my wife and I have had the privilege to know fellowship with my Baptist brothers, Independent brothers, Pentecostal brothers, and Presbyterian brothers. My wife grew up Grace Brethren and we have many friends in the Christian Missionary Alliance Church as well.

And in all of those settings, I have never been to one congregation where the people of God did not claim promises for their covenant children. It was not always taught as such, but it was nevertheless seen. The reason is because God's covenant with us brings *the Life of Christ* to us and this has implications for our children.

And because baptism is the New Testament covenant sign, the covenant nature of what this sign represents inevitably comes to expression regardless of the particular church or denomination represented. *God's DNA* cannot help but express *Life*. That's what Peter said, "For the promise is for you and your children and for all who are far off-for all whom the Lord our God will call" (Acts 2:39).

How do we see God's DNA expressed to our kids?

As a pastor I have baptized covenant children for the past 25 years. I have observed *God's DNA* coming to expression regardless of the different theologies. God's Life will prevail!

Some of my brothers dedicate their kids to God by a public dedication service with the parents and the kids coming forward to ask the blessing of God to be placed upon the kids as Jesus is quoted in saying, "Let the little children come to me, and do not hinder them, for the kingdom of heaven belongs to such as these" (Matthew 19:14).

But this is not the only passage quoted. My brothers do not just find justification in dedicating the little ones of believers to the Lord in the New Testament. They also appeal to the Old Testament where Hannah dedicated Samuel to the Lord (1st Samuel 1:28).

Brothers who baptize their children also go back to the Old Testament for the basis of what they do. But instead of using Hannah's example of dedicating Samuel to the Lord, they appeal to what happened when God made his covenant with Abraham. God said that his covenant with Abraham would have implications for Abraham's children. "I will establish my covenant as an everlasting covenant between me and you and your descendents after you for the generations to come, to be your God and the God of your descendants after you" (Genesis 17:17).

Both those who dedicate their kids and those who baptize them appeal to the Old Testament promises and what they see as New Testament practices. They disagree, sometimes violently (☺) with how these things should be applied, but they all see the principle that God wants to bless our kids and they pray for them by either dedicating them or baptizing them in a public worship service.

Neither those who dedicate nor those who baptize believe that what they have done will guarantee the salvation of the child. But they both pray that God will be merciful and that one day the parents will be able to look back and remember this day as the time that they gave their kids to Jesus.

There really is a connection between God's covenant promises and us!

In speaking of the significance of what Christ does in our lives, Paul makes the connection between these two covenant signs when he writes to the church at Colosse. "For in Christ all the fullness of the Deity lives in bodily form, and you have been given fullness in Christ, who is the head over every power and authority. In him you were also circumcised, in the putting off of the sinful nature, not with a *circumcision* done by the hands of men but with the *circumcision* done by Christ, having been buried with him in *baptism* and raised with him through your faith in the power of God, who raised him from the dead" (NIV Colossians 2:9-12 translation; italics are mine).

Note that Paul says, in essence, that God has given us his *DNA, his Dynamic Nucleus Activity,* because we have been given, "fullness in Christ!" This is an awesome statement since in Christ, "all the fullness of the Deity lives in bodily form" (Colossians 2:9).

So what is happening in believers is something that God is doing at what I call a *spiritually genetic level.* God is working in our souls and in the process his presence is transforming our lives. This transformation, this *DNA transformation,* cannot lay dormant in us or in our ministries as his Body. *God's Life* will express itself in our *Life in Christ.*

This means that regardless of our theological position, we are dealing with what is happening in our lives as a result of *God's work in us.* Paul confirms that God is making a covenant with us by what Christ does in our lives. Christ spiritually circumcises our hearts and he unites us to his death and resurrection through a spiritual baptism (Colossians 2:12).

It is *God* who has called us. It is *God* who has saved us in Jesus. It is *God* who has poured out his *Spirit* into our lives (Acts 2:30—39). And his *DNA* cannot but help be expressed in our lives anymore than you can stop a man being changed who has just been raised from the dead!

You can't escape the impact of God's making covenant with us even if you only baptize professing adults. You have still placed *God's covenant sign* on them and that will have *covenant* implications for their children! You will feel compelled to do something to bring your kids into a relationship with Jesus because you will innately feel that God's love extends to your kids. You will either baptize them or dedicate them, but you will find yourself bringing them to Jesus and asking that Jesus bring them to himself.

We are called to express God's DNA of grace!

I know my brothers who feel strongly about not baptizing their children do so because of their conviction that baptism is for "believers only." But when they dedicate their children to God they are expressing an innate manifestation of God's covenant. The reason is because at some level we all get that it's never just about us. We know that God loves our loved ones and delights to work in them. So we want to do something to commit them to God and ask for his mercy upon them.

In a similar way, we see the apostle Paul applying God's covenant promises to marriage by telling believers they are not to divorce their unbelieving spouses because, they are nevertheless "sanctified" by them (1st Corinthians 7:12-14). And we see in that same context Paul reminding believers that if they leave their marriages, when their unbelieving partners want to stay married, that they will have a negative impact on their kids. "Otherwise your children would be unclean, but as it is, they are holy" (1st Corinthians 7:14). So if your unbelieving spouse wants to continue to live with you in marriage, do so knowing that it will have a covenantal impact on your spouse and your kids! God will continue to work but you are called to trust him for the work he needs to do.

Don't let the love of God be lost in how we say it to others!

Neither those who dedicate their children nor those who have their children baptized believe that the particular service "saves" their kids. Both teach and believe that God's *Spirit* must do the saving work in their kids if they are to come to a personal relationship with Jesus. Both take vows, both have times of prayer for the kids and the parents. Both ask the congregations to be involved in the lives of the kids and help the parents by encouraging them on their journey in Jesus.

My point is that God's *DNA* does come to express itself. It comes to expression when we submit ourselves to baptism to demonstrate our own allegiance to Jesus. And it comes to expression as we seek God's *Spirit* to be gracious and *be poured out in our children* as he has been *poured out in our lives*. "For the promise is for you and your children and for all who are far off-for all whom the Lord our God will call" (Acts 2:39).

The promise of God to be a covenant keeping God to our families will express itself regardless of anyone's personal denominational background. And frankly, I think that anything that gets though our denominational filters must be of *the Spirit!* Remember it was God who said, "The promise is for you and your children!" This is not some well-wishing on our part. It is the promise of God! So claim it! Rejoice in it! But don't be divided over it!

You see the thing of it is, while we battle for our view of "baptism" there is something far grander happening. God is actually saving people! He is rescuing people from the kingdom of darkness and bringing them into the grace and freedom that are ours in Jesus! He is pouring out his Spirit into the lives of his people and he is coming to express his life DNA qualities in their lives . . . sometimes despite us!

When you see these things coming to express themselves in the lives of God's people, you know that God's *Dynamic Nucleus Activity, his DNA*, is present within the church. *New Life* has come because have been given of *"the fullness of the Christ."* Baptism is an outward sign of that spiritual reality. When God is doing more and more in *the Life of his Church*, we will be seeing more and more baptisms (Matthew 28:19-20)! It is part of his *DNA!*

Consider taking a fresh look at the importance of "Baptism"

1. First of all you need to consider whether you have been baptized? If you haven't this is *the next step* you need to take. Read Matthew 28:18-20

2. Secondly, if you were publically received into a local church, were you asked to share your testimony before the congregation? If you were, did that make you feel uncomfortable or excited about the opportunity to share what God was doing in your life? Read Luke 9:21-27 and consider, "Was Christ ashamed of you? What did Jesus do for you that you might be presented whole and forgiven before God?"

3. Lastly, if you have never publically shared your faith consider writing out a short testimony to help you think about what you would say if you were asked.

   Include three things in your testimony:

   a. What was your life like before you came to Christ?

   b. How did you come to know Jesus as your personal Savior?

   c. What difference has it made in your life now that you know Him?

If you came to know Jesus when you were a little child you may not remember a time when you never knew Jesus. How blessed you are! Have you thought about the benefits of coming to know Jesus as a child? Write out your testimony describing the benefits of knowing Jesus from an early age and think about who God used to most influence your life. Take time to pray and thank God for them! This is your testimony and thinking through it will help you be able to share your faith when you are asked.

If you became a believer later in life, your life will certainly be different now! Think about what your life was like before you became a Christian. Then write out a brief paragraph about what God did to bring you to himself. He may have used a friend in your life, it may have been a family member, or it may have been a Gideon Bible in a motel! But your testimony will be special because it is yours! Then conclude thinking about your testimony by writing out some ways that Jesus has changed your life. This is also an important part of showing why life in Christ really does express itself by Life and it is important to be able to share that with others.

If you are on a journey in Jesus it will become obvious and people will ask you why your life is different. So think about your testimony and be prepared to tell people why knowing Jesus has meant so much to you.

Read 1 Peter 3:15 and think about how you can share your faith, "with gentleness and respect." But do it!

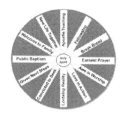

Chapter 5
God's DNA:
Welcome to God's Family

There is nothing more affirming than to be genuinely welcomed into a family as though you should have been there all along. Some of you have experienced this by being welcomed into a friend's family as though you were a son or daughter. Some may have experienced this when welcomed into the family of your future spouse. But hopefully all of you have known this from joining the fellowship of a local church.

I really pray that when you joined a congregation for the first time, you were made to feel that you were as welcome as if you had been born there. We all came from the same "womb" as the Spirit of God brought eternal life to us (John 3:7). We all have the same heavenly Father though we may have been "born" in different cities (Romans 8:15). So being part of the same spiritual family, having the same spiritual *DNA* at work in us, we ought to be accepting to one another and receive new believers into the family as our brothers and sisters in Christ (1st Corinthians 12:13).

But if the church forgets her "birthplace," if she forgets that it was God who gave her Life, she starts living as though she gave birth to herself! She becomes arrogant thinking she is doing God a great favor to be his child. And when that happens, she starts acting as if others need to measure up before they can be welcomed into the *their* church family.

Do we come together to celebrate or to act as members of a club?

If the church was a club, it would be ok to check out who measured up to your membership standards and decide among yourselves who should and who should not be admitted. But she isn't a club. Proof of that is in the fact that no one in God's church ever measured up to his standards (Psalm 51:5).

We are in her because we have been personally invited by Jesus. He has said, "Come to me, all you who are weary and burdened, and I will give you rest" (Matthew 11:28). And we have come to Jesus and found that his words of rest are true! He has given us his Holy Spirit who has marked us as God's and sealed us for eternity so that we cannot be denied what he has purchased for us on the cross (Ephesians 1:13-14).

Grace is never credentialed!

Grace is never a credentialed acceptance. "For all have sinned and fall short of the glory of God" (Romans 3:23). Every time we try and make it so we find that we no longer have grace at work among us. In fact, we find ourselves becoming less and less gracious with others. The reason is because we feel compelled to do more and more to maintain our credentials and yet we find it does less and less for us in our relationship with God. So the only alternative we have to just living in our own misery is to make others as miserable as we are.

That's not a very nice thing to do. And it's especially inappropriate in the church. The church is to be the one place of refuge where any sinner can flee to knowing that he can escape from any avenger who would have him condemned and find acceptance from those who have never met him before.

It is to be the one place where people understand how all of us get in trouble at times. The reason is because all who are in the fellowship of God's people know that they too are sinners. So it is not hard at all to accept other sinners into their fellowship.

That's why God's people daily confess to him their own sins. We are all in need of cleansing and renewal. We all need to be refreshed in the well of Living Water (John 4:10). Otherwise, as some of my Australian brothers say, "We find ourselves sucking mud."

The same horror that you see others' sin bring is the same horror that you feel about your own sin. And you are either free to admit that or you force others to pretend with you. And if that is the case, you have lied to yourselves because it will be quite obvious to others that understand grace that you have forgotten what grace is. The apostle John says, "If we claim to be without sin, we deceived ourselves and the truth is not in us" (1 John 1:8). So why would we pretend that we are better than we are? Why would we want to do that and put ourselves in the position of having to keep up appearances? Why not instead fall at the cross and admit your desperate need of Jesus? And when you do so, it will not be hard for you to accept others who are desperate for him too.

Clubs protect their membership from outsiders, Jesus welcomes them!

Are we afraid of others being favored by the same Lord who favored us? Are we jealous of others having more "gifts" to offer than we do? Are we afraid of no longer having the positions of power that we presently have? What if others join that don't share in our history or have our vision for ministry? Are we jealous for God or for our own selfish desires?

Either the church is a family of God or it isn't. And if it is God's family, he is the one who decides who will be coming! Our calling is to welcome, accept, and challenge each others in our journeys in Jesus. Jesus has already spread out his arms on the cross to welcome whomever he chooses to call. How can we keep our arms from embracing them too? Don't we realize that if we don't embrace them as our brothers and sisters in Jesus, that we are also missing out on getting Jesus' embrace of us through them?

What does our "welcome" say about us?

Have you considered the fact that how we "welcome" others into the family of God actually says as much about us as it does about those to whom we are commanded to love and accept and encourage on their journey? So I pray that you have been "welcomed well" into a family of God because you have every right to know how awesome it is that God has so loved us that He has made us equal heirs with Christ! "The Spirit testifies with our spirit that we are God's children. Now if we are children, then we are heirs-heirs of God and co-heirs with Christ" (Romans 8:16-17).

I also pray that you will now be among others who "welcome well" those who come to your fellowship for encouragement. Paul said to Philemon that he should even welcome his runaway slave because he was now returning to him as a believer. "So if you consider me a partner, welcome him as you would welcome me" (Philemon 1:17).

It has often been said that you don't get a second chance at a first impression. Well, you don't get a second chance at a first welcome either. And I pray that the next time you have the opportunity to "welcome" a new believer into God's family, or the next time you have the privilege of "welcoming" a believer into your fellowship that has just moved into your area and "joined," I pray that you will welcome them with the arms of Jesus openly extended and heart exposed to accept them as part of your own family.

What baptism says publically to the world about a believer's commitment, being welcomed into God's family says privately to the individual's soul that their commitment will be worth it because no matter what happens, they have a new family that will help them, encourage them, pray for them, support them, and challenge them to remain faithful and full of joy on their journey in Jesus. It tells them they have a new home and this one will be there for eternity. So give them a "welcome" that will be worthy of that!

How were people "welcomed" in the Book of Acts?

There are a number of examples in Acts about how this played out in the early church. Sometimes there were shining examples of what the church should be like. At other times, well to be honest, the "welcome" stank. But we can learn from all of these and grow from them.

Let's start with the good stuff first!

In Acts 2, when Christ poured out the Holy Spirit upon the church, there was an incredible "welcome" to new believers by the exiting church. It was obvious that these new brethren had also come under *conviction* for their sins at Peter's preaching (Acts 2:37). It was also obvious that they were willing to take whatever *next steps* they needed to take in their journey in Jesus, because they wholeheartedly submitted to being *baptized* (Acts 2:41), unafraid of what persecution such a public step may bring. And it was equally obvious that having submitted to baptism that they were immediately added to the church and *"welcomed"* by her without reservation. Luke records for us that, "Those who accepted the message were baptized and about three thousand were added to their number that day" (Acts 2:41).

No one said, "Do we really want these guys?"

No one sat down and said, "Do you guys really think this is a good idea?" "Is anybody else worried about the fact that this is going to draw attention to us by the Roman government?" "Don't you think that having just crucified our 'Leader' and 'Lord,' that they might be just the tiniest bit interested in taking care of the rest of us?" "Aren't you worried that they might want to crush what looks to be an open and growing rebellion?"

No one said, "What are we going to do with these 3,000 new members?" "They don't know as much as we do; they haven't been part of our small group or personal life journeys; they don't know our confession and haven't taken the membership class; why Peter isn't scheduled to teach one for another three years!" "And where are we supposed to hold worship services?" "We can't fit all these new members into the synagogue, why it will even be a squeeze in the coliseum!" "Why we don't even have their names yet!" "They didn't sign any visitor's card and no one knows where they live!" "How are we going to have a follow-up ministry with all these people?" "We were struggling with our 120!" "What are we going to do now?"

No one said, "And what if they have needs?" "Well, Duh?" "We can't possibly feed a bunch like this!" "I move that we take back their membership and have a think about this before it gets too far!"

Thank God that wasn't the attitude of the early church leaders! And we have testimony that it wasn't the response of the early church family either. They welcomed the new believers and invited them into their lives! "They devoted themselves to the apostles' teaching and to fellowship, to the breaking of bread and to prayer. Everyone was filled with awe, and many wonders and miraculous signs were done by the apostles. All the believers were together and had everything in common. Selling their possessions and goods, they gave to anyone as he had need" (Acts 2:42-45).

Man! Talk about a "welcome!" Talk about being received as family! There is no doubt that these early believers really did, "get it!" And it didn't come as a result of a committee or conference or character profile! It came as a result of their being aware of what Jesus had done for each of them and how that now made them all brothers and sisters in the family of God.

After all, weren't they doing what real families ought to do? Weren't they willing to learn and find their place in the family by listening to the apostles' teaching? Weren't they acting as a family by eating together? Weren't they acting as a family by financially helping one another whenever there was a need?

These brethren led the way in showing us what it really means to "welcome" other believers into the Family of God! And this was expressing God's DNA for it demonstrated visibly how they had been accepted spiritually by God himself.

How not to "welcome" people!

There are other examples in the early church that aren't so exemplary. Like when some of the widows of Greek descent were overlooked by those more concerned about caring for widows of Israeli heritage (Acts 6:1). Like when even Ananias and the apostles didn't want to accept that something genuine had happened to Saul on the road to Damascus. They feared this former persecutor of the church and at first didn't want to welcome him (Acts 9:13, 14, 26). And then there was Peter's struggle to believe that Gentiles, like Cornelius, could be of equal standing before God as any Jew because of Jesus. He had to go on his own pilgrimage to faith in this area of his life and then try and convince others that they had also been blinded about the implications of really believing that Christ accepts both Jew and Gentile alike (Acts 10:9-11:18). Eventually this called for the church to hold its first assembly to deal with the issue of how to welcome all the Gentiles who were coming to faith in Christ (Acts 15:1-35).

There have been shining examples of believers "welcoming" others into their fellowship, but there were other examples were new believers were treated callously with suspicion. Others were treated shamefully with outright rejection.

The New Testament is honest about this and we need to be honest about our lives as well. We have both recorded for us in the Bible so that we might see just how important it is to "welcome" others who have come to faith in Christ, or who have joined us in their journey in Jesus.

The way we "welcome" others is itself a sign of just what we understand of the gospel: God loves sinners, and welcomes all who come to Him through His Son without showing partiality! "Accept one another, then, just as Christ accepted you" (Romans 15:7)! "There is one body and one Spirit-just as you were called to one hope when you were called-one Lord, one faith, one baptism; one God and Father of all, who is over all and through all and in all" (Ephesians 4:4-5). "For through Him we both have access to the Father by one Spirit" (Ephesians 2:18).

Remember, God takes "welcomes" seriously. "If people do not *welcome you*, shake the dust off your feet when you leave their town, as a testimony against them" (Luke 9:5). I don't know about you, but I don't want to be one who has failed to "welcome" those God has brought to us. It says more about us, than it says about them!

So "welcome" one another into the Family of God and see what God will do as you learn to grow together in his grace. It is one of the *DNA* characteristics of the *Spirit's Life* among us! You can't grow as a church family unless you let your family go through all the struggles of learning to love one another as Jesus has loved us. Clubs can avoid that and resend membership. God's family is forever!

Consider how being "Welcomed" or "Not being Welcomed" impacted you

1. Most of the horror stories I have heard over the years about churches have started on how they have *"welcomed"* new people. If you have had a horrible experience and been hurt by not being made to feel that you were really important to God and the people of God in your church, there is probably not much you

can do to change your church's policy. But one thing you can do is to start a new approach yourself. Get involved with the *"Greeters Ministry"* in your church and by your life make a difference to the new people that God brings to that ministry.

2. Pray for the ministry that you are involved in. Ask *the Holy Spirit* to make it the kind of ministry that makes people feel *"welcome"* from the time they come until in the providence of God they move to another area.

3. Try and find ways to network with other believers in other churches in your area so that *your city* becomes a *"Welcoming Ministry"* to people who move to your area. Don't forget that ministry takes place one person at a time and your reaching out to others will make a difference for Jesus where you live.

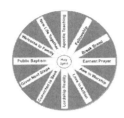

Chapter 6
God's DNA: New Life Together

We were created to be in relationships.

Before time, from all eternity, God existed in relationship as Father, Son and Holy Spirit. This ought to immediately tell us that healthy relationships are not an option of our existence for they are at the heart of our being created in the very image of God. After all God did say, "Let us make man in our image," and that's exactly what God did (Genesis 1:26, 27)!

In that creation directive flowing from the discussion of God, there came the immediate implication of that directive that, "in the image of God He created him; male and female He created them," that it, "was not good for the man to be alone," so He created him a, "helper suitable for him" (Genesis 1:27; 2:18).

The Fellowship of the Trinity created the Fellowship of Humanity because man was created in God's image. And this reflection of God's image in man determined that we should live life together, not alone; for God himself spoke and said, "It is not good for the man to be alone."

Now there are lots of reasons why we may end up trying to make the effort to live life alone. But we need to see that God's original design was for us to live life and enjoy life together in relationships. I want to say more about this when we get to the chapter dealing with "Fellowship," but I felt it critical for us to see that God's DNA of living life together came from our creative design. We were created for relationships.

Why do we have dysfunctional relationships?

It would be good to note here that it was sin that first introduced the difficulty, indeed, impossibility to live life together without grace. When Adam and Eve chose to eat of the Tree of Knowledge of Good and Evil, despite God's explicit command that they not do so, their action introduced sin into the world (Genesis 2:15-16; 3:1-7). This became the root of our alienation from God and one another. This created dysfunctional relationships.

Adam and Eve suddenly found themselves alienated from God, for when they heard God walking in the cool of the Garden of Eden they hid from him (Genesis 3:8). When God confronted them as to why they were hiding, Adam blamed God and then he blamed Eve. What he didn't do was accept blame himself.

Adam said, "The woman you put here with me-she gave me some fruit from the tree, and I ate it," thus blaming God for giving him the type of wife that he gave him. And he blamed Eve for placing the fruit in his hands (Genesis 3:12). At no point did Adam acknowledge his sin and that in itself was sinful because he denied his own culpability.

Eve didn't fare any better. The woman also shifted blame saying, "The serpent deceived me, and I ate" (Genesis 3:12). Eve as much as blamed God as Adam did for the implication is that if God had not created the serpent, she wouldn't have been deceived into her disobedience either. Thus, Eve joined her husband in denying any part of her own responsibility and this severed her relationship with God and her husband.

It brought "dysfunctional" into our life language. Satan had introduced Adam and Eve to sin and they had experienced the broken relationships that immediately flowed out of it. They had been alienated from God and each other.

For any hope of reconciliation to come, God would have to take the initiative because sin had now been introduced into God's creation and man was incapable of providing a remedy. Sin introduced a *spiritually corrupt dna* into their nature. It was not the Spirit of God moving in their lives, but it became *the spirit of this age*. Paul says describes this as, *"the spirit who is now at work in those who are disobedient"* (Ephesians 2:2, emphasis mine).

Adam and Eve were the first to experience this corruption of their natures. Their *spiritually corrupt dna (dysfunctional nucleus activity of the flesh)* became the source of the way in which men would now respond to God and to one another. It would also become the source of *genetically corrupt* information that would form the way in which they would respond to the earth. They would rebel against God, they would seek their own way in their relationships with each other, and they would abuse the earth God had given them to care for. The change in their *spiritual dna* would become obvious.

Eve's spiritual corruption would now hinder her if she tried to fulfill her calling. Two examples of this are her increased pain of childbearing and her desire to now dominate her husband. Her increased pain at child bearing would set her against the desire to have children. No longer would there be joy in hearing, "Be fruitful and multiply" (Genesis 1:28).

And the second consequence of her sin would be the desire to rule over her husband instead of supporting him (Genesis 2:18; 3:16). Later Solomon would say, "Better to live on a corner of the roof than share a house with a quarrelsome wife" (Proverbs 25:24). A husband needs the love and support of his wife. He doesn't need to feel that she is trying to control him.

Women don't realize how much power they already have over their husbands. But that power can so easily be used against their husbands instead of being a source of strength to them. Grace is needed for women to discover their value to God and to their husbands. They don't have to seek power, they already have power! The thing is, like men, we don't enjoy real life unless our life is coming from Jesus. And for that we need the Spirit to be at work in us transforming us at the very core of our spiritual natures.

Adam's *corrupt dna* would include his inability to deal with Eve in a loving and godly way. He would no longer see his wife as his comforter but as his competitor (Genesis 2:18; 3:16). She would try and rule over him instead of supporting him (Ephesians 5:22).

Eve had literally come from Adam's side, and she should have remained close to his heart forever (Genesis 2:22). But now Adam would be glad to get out of the house to go and work in the garden!

There was a problem, however, for he wouldn't have relief there either. Weeds would try and squeeze the life out of any of his labor. And in so doing, they would now try and rule over him where Adam had originally been created to rule over them (Genesis 1:28-29; 3:17-19).

Eve would have pain in the birthing of children. Adam would have pain in the birthing of a harvest because thorns and thistles and sweat would now be required if he was to fulfill his calling (Genesis 3:18-19). They had sinned and that sin had brought alienation from God, each other, and the earth. But that was not the end of their dysfunction relationships.

Adam and Eve's first sons would experience the impacts of their parents' fall into sin. Cain, their firstborn, would kill Abel, his brother (Genesis 4:8). The consequences of this action continue to day with the violence of men and their enmity against one another.

All of this came upon the earth because Adam and Eve chose to disobey God. The relationships they were created to enjoy and share became filled with contradictions, difficulties, alienations, and even death because they were no longer in a relationship with God unmarred by sin. Their *spiritual dna* had been *corrupted* and was in need of redemption.

Dysfunctional relationships transformed into Dynamic relationships!

The gospel affirms God's determination to not let the condition of man end in the brokenness of what they had experienced in their relationships. We see this first promised to even Adam and Eve for God said to Satan, "And I will put enmity between you and the woman, and between your offspring and hers; he will crush your head, and you will strike his heel" (Genesis 3:15).

Centuries later Isaiah prophesied of Christ that, "But he was pierced for our transgressions, he was crushed for our iniquities; the punishment that brought us peace was upon him, and by his wounds we are healed" (Isaiah 53:5). This meant that we are healed even in our relationships.

The apostle Paul showed how even the differences between Jews and Gentiles were now resolved through the death of Christ. "For he himself is our peace, who has made the two one and has destroyed the barrier, the dividing wall of hostility, by abolishing in his flesh the law with its commandments and regulations. His purpose was to create in himself one new man out of the two, thus making peace, and in this one body to reconcile both of them to God through the cross, by which he put to death their hostility" (Ephesians 2:14-16).

This means that in Christ we are reconciled to God and enabled to live a new reconciled life with others. We have individually received in *new life in Christ*, but this joins us to *the new life* that others have come to experience in him as well. To put it another way, having been reconciled to God through Christ's death on the cross for us, we cannot help but pursue reconciliation with others because God has restored us to the DNA of our created design: *To live in dynamic relationships with God and each other.*

As the apostle Paul puts it, "We were therefore buried with him through baptism into death in order that, just as Christ was raised from the dead, through the glory of the Father, we too may live *a new life*" (Romans 6:4). And you cannot separate the *Life of Christ* that the *Holy Spirit* has poured out into us from the *Life of Christ* that the *Holy Spirit* has poured out into other believers. It's not just that as individuals God gives us a *new life*, through that is true. But it is also that God gives us *new life* together so that, "we too may live a new life" (Romans 6:4).

Dysfunctional churches need the Dynamic power of God's Spirit!

It is impossible for us to have this *new life* together apart from *the Spirit of God*. Whenever people get together and try to be together and enjoy one another's company, inevitably sin will come up! And when sin arises, so does the alienation that we feel.

The apostle Paul describes this as living out of our "flesh" because it is life in the raw apart from *the Spirit's life* in us. We do what comes "naturally" and it only in the end produces spiritual cancer. You know what this looks like in community because you see divisions, selfish ambitions, jealousies, and the like.

And if we are honest, we will admit that it doesn't happen to only non-Christians. Paul pointed out that the church at Corinth had returned to their *corrupt dna* when he said that they were living as though they were not Christians; as though God had not done anything in their lives. Instead they were living as "worldly" believers; as believers who did nothing except what came naturally.

"Brothers, I could not address you as spiritual but as worldly-mere infants in Christ. I gave you milk, not solid food, for you were not yet ready for it. Indeed you are still not ready. You are still worldly. For since there is jealousy and quarreling among you, are you not worldly? Are you not acting as mere men" (1st Corinthians 3:1-3)?

This is like having corrupt *dna of the flesh* and it manifests itself as a *dysfunctional cell* in the Body of Christ causing all the healthy cells around it to be tainted by its unhealthy characteristics. Paul speaks of this type of corruption that can affect the Body of Christ when he speaks with a severe warning, "The acts of the sinful nature are obvious: sexual immorality, impurity and debauchery; idolatry and witchcraft; hatred, discord, jealousy, fits of rage, selfish ambition, dissensions, factions and envy; drunkenness, orgies, and the like. I warn you, as I did before, that those who live like this will not inherit the kingdom of God" (Galatians 5:19-21).

But it doesn't have to be this way. We see what happened at *Pentecost* when God poured out his Spirit upon his church. Believers were united and filled with joy as they lived out of *the new life* they had received in Christ. In contrast to *the corrupt dna* that we naturally had before our conversion, God gives us his Spirit which produces *a new DNA* in us as believers, impacting our life together as a healthy Body of Christ. "But the fruit of the Spirit is love, joy, peace, patience, kindness, goodness, faithfulness, gentleness and self control. Against such things there is no law. Those who belong to Christ Jesus have crucified the sinful nature with its passions and desires" (Galatians 5:22-24).

Only for God's DNA to be manifested, we have to realize that there is a real spiritual war going on and we are going to need the Spirit of God to bring about Christ's victory in our lives. When as believers we cry out for mercy and God shows it by restoring us to a relationship with Him, it must spill over into our seeing restoration in relationships with others. And we will experience God's *DNA* of *New Life Together* as we "keep in step with in the Spirit" (Galatians 5:25).

Believers have all been made to drink from the same Spirit, having the same Lord, and same Father in heaven (1st Corinthians 12:12-13; Ephesians 4:4-5). And it was now impossible for us to not be experiencing a desire to be working out their relationships with each other. "No one who is born of God will continue to sin, because *God's seed* remains in him" (1 John 3:9).

Consequently, the apostle John challenged believers, "Do not be like Cain, who belonged to the evil one and murdered his brother . . . We know that we have passed from death to life, because we love our brothers" (1 John 3:12, 14). John's point is that if "God's seed remains" in you, you can't possibly pursue a life that reflects the hatred that Cain expressed in the murdering of his brother.

Or, to put it in the metaphor I have been using, if *God's DNA* is at work in your life, to do anything less than to love your brother is inconsistent with the new life that is now at work in you, the God-Life, *because you have a spiritually different DNA at work in you!*

God's Spirit brings God's Life to us!

So constitutive is this manifestation of *God's DNA* to us that John says, "Everyone who believes that Jesus is the Christ is born of God, and everyone who loves the father loves his child as well" (1 John 5:1). The *new life* that we have from God manifests itself in the *new life* that we begin to see within the family of God.

We were created to be in relationships. It is in our *spiritual DNA*. God had lived in relationship as the Father, Son, and Spirit from all eternity. So when he created us in his image, it would inevitably be part of our creative design. Our *created DNA* is that we live in relationship. We are created to live in a right relationship with God and in a right relationship with others. This is part of our *spiritually genetic code*. It was corrupted at the fall when Adam sinned against God. But it has been restored through Christ for all who come to God through him. *His shed blood* has become our *redemptive DNA*.

God's DNA come to us through Christ's shed blood!

In the Old Testament, when sacrifices were made the blood was to be poured out because, *"the blood is the life"* (Deuteronomy 12:23). God spoke through Moses to instruct the people, "For the life of a creature is in the blood, and I have given it to you to make atonement for yourselves on the altar; it is the blood that makes atonement for one's life (Leviticus 17:11).

Think about that! It is the blood that makes atonement because *the blood is the life*. All of the Old Testament sacrifices pointed to the one sacrifice of Jesus! It was his shed blood that atoned for our sins. "In fact, the law requires that nearly everything be cleansed with blood, and without the shedding of blood there is no forgiveness" (Hebrews 9:22). "How much more, then, will the blood of Christ, who through the eternal Spirit offered himself unblemished to God, cleanse our consciences from acts that lead to death, so that we may serve the living God" (Hebrews 9:14).

So through Jesus' blood we have life! When making this point to those who had been following him, Jesus said to them, "Whoever eats my flesh and drinks my blood has eternal life, and I will raise him up at the last day" (John 6:54). There was not a literal partaking of his flesh or blood in view. He was referring to a spiritual participation and union that believers would come to know with him as the Holy Spirit brought Christ's life to them by applying the benefits of his death to them.

But this shows the origin of God's DNA as being from the very blood of Jesus poured out for us on Calvary's cross. This life we received from him as he poured out his life upon us when he poured out his *Spirit* at Pentecost!

And it is God's *Spirit* who brings *Jesus' Life* to us with its *spiritual DNA* and all of its power to transform us including not only our relationship with God, but also our relationships with each other.

That's why no believer can be indifferent about what is happening in his relationships with others. If we have God's DNA at work in us, if his *Spirit* is moving in our lives, by definition, *by spiritual union with Christ,* we have to see *the Life of Jesus* manifesting itself in *how we live Life together* because we have all had his *Life blood* applied to our lives. It is Christ's blood that makes us brothers because we all receive eternal life from his sacrifice.

God's DNA will manifest itself in relationships!

John says that so intrinsic is this life that we have in Christ to the life that we share with others, that if *Christ's Life* is not seen in our relationships with others, we don't have life with God either! "If anyone says, 'I love God,' yet hates his brother, he is a liar" (1 John 4:20).

We see the dynamic power of this *new life together* as lived out by the early church. In Acts 2 believers evidenced *Christ's Life* together by their lives being changed by *the Life of Christ in them.* It is obvious that the effect of his crucifixation became the life force in their lives as they experienced the power of his shed blood. Christ's blood is put to the account of sinners so that their blood will not be required of them. He literally pays the debt that sinners owe God because of breaking God's law. As Paul says, "God made him who had to sin to be sin for us, so that in him we might become the righteousness of God" (2nd Corinthians 5:21). And since believers have "crossed over from death to life" because of Jesus, life is now seen in them (John 5:24).

In Acts we see believers showing this *Life* by the way they studied the apostles' teaching and had fellowship together as one. They prayed together and then worked out what their prayers meant as they in genuine and real ways helped each other financially. There was no one in need among them because they saw that *the Life* they had in Christ was a *Life* that they had *together* in Christ.

The only thing that would threaten this life would be the introduction of sin into their midst. Paul warned the Roman believers to be careful about guarding *the new life* that they were enjoying together in Christ, "I urge you, brothers, to watch out for those who cause divisions and put obstacles in your way that are contrary to the teaching you have learned. Keep away from them. For such people are not serving our Lord Christ, but their own appetites. By smooth talk and flattery they deceive the minds of naïve people. Everyone has heard about your obedience, so I am full of joy over you; but I want you to be wise about what is good and innocent about what is evil. The God of peace will soon crush Satan under your feet" (Romans 16:17-20).

Paul showed how divisions in relationships came from what Satan did in the Garden when he deceived Eve (Genesis 3:15). Yet because of the power of the shed blood of Jesus now put to their account, *the Life* God had given them in Christ, Paul encouraged them by saying that, "the God of peace will soon crush Satan under your feet."

He said this because he knew that what God does in the lives of his people cannot be stopped! *God's redemptive DNA* in the blood of Jesus will overcome any *corrupt dna (dysfunctional nucleus activity of the flesh)* in the life of the worse of sinners!

The believers of Rome were experiencing *new life* together. It was reflective of being restored to God, reconciled to Him through the death of His Son. So he warned them to guard that *new life* together and not let men divide them.

The *Life* given us by *the Holy Spirit*, not only *"births us spiritually,"* it continues to cause us to *"grow spiritually,"* thus demonstrating the reality that we have come to personally experience what Jesus said, "I have come that they might have *life*, and have it to the full" (John 3:7-8; 6:33, 45; 10:10).

Note that this *Life* comes to us together, "that *they* might have *life*." Also note that it is a full life; an abundant one which in the Greek means, "exceeding some number, or measure, or rank, or need."[3]

And this life is to be lived out in not only our relationship with God but in our relationships with others. God has called us to know this *"God-Life"* with one another.

Christianity isn't just a bunch of believers who are either "Survivors" (barely getting along with one another), or "Winners" (who try to beat each other)!

We are called to be brothers and sisters in God's Family who share our lives together! We see this happening at Pentecost as believers came together and shared in the apostles' teaching, and in fellowship and in breaking of bread and prayer together in one another's homes. They even shared their wealth with one another so that no one was in need.

There will always be times of great sorrow as well as times of great joy. But it is in the sharing of these things together that we are enriched and experience more of Christ's Life.

---

[3]   Definition from BibleWorks 6, copy write 2003

Live Life as those who have God's Redemptive DNA at work in them!

I used to think that knowing Jesus was pretty much about just being forgiven. Now that's a very good place to start, but that is what it is . . . only the beginning! When God calls us to himself he gives us his Spirit so that our lives will actually be changed.

I have used *the DNA metaphor* to show how extensive this change is. We will have a better life because we know God's forgiveness, but our lives will be so much more because *Christ's Life* is now at work in us.

What God is doing in our lives, as a result of his *Spirit* being at work in us, far exceeds anything we could ever imagine! *God's DNA* is going to manifest itself at the deepest levels of our lives and his *Spirit* is going to transform us according to who God is fashioning us to be. Paul says, "Though outwardly we are wasting away, yet inwardly we are being renewed day by day" (2nd Corinthians 4:16).

It isn't Rocket Science . . . it is so much more!

When I was a teenage, I used to build model rockets with my best friend Dale Ward. It was so cool! We would buy the kits and make the rockets with our own ideas being worked into our projects. And after lots of care and anxious energy for the launch, the day would come and we would try and find an open field to light them up!

Comparing a life that you can experience just knowing that you are forgiven as compared to a *Life* that you can know realizing that *God's Spirit is alive in you* is kind of like saying that Dale and I were NASA Rocket Scientists!

Granted, we may have thought we were, but in our early days we didn't let too many people know what we were doing because our launches didn't always go, shall we say, "Smoothly!"

Building model rockets, sanding down the fins to get the angles right, installing from one to five engines to power those beauties was awesome. But the rush came when we touched the ignition wire to the car battery! A whiff of smoke and they were away!

Sometimes so were we! We had to run for cover more than once! One of the multiple engines rockets only had one engine to fire. It made it past the three foot pole launch rod, but then leaned sideways before the other three engines kicked in! Apart from being afraid that it was going to hit Dale's car when it blasted across the field, it was a rush!

We had such a cool time, we really did! Even when we had to chase some of the rockets for miles because the wind pushed their parachute descent far from our launch zone!

But as cool as that was, it is nothing compared to living in Florida and watching a Space Shuttle launch in the evening sky! Now I've done that with my wife and I can tell you that it beats anything Dale and I ever made!

God's Spirit launches us into His Mission for our lives!

But the thing is that we don't seem to realize that there is an even greater difference between the 'life' that we can live apart from God, and the *"Life"* we can have *in Christ*, who through *the Holy Spirit*, brings *his Life* to dwell within us.

We who were formerly living life out of the consequences of our own sin; and out of the consequences of others' sin impacting us; and out of the consequences of sin's impact upon the world; and we who were estranged from God and from others; we are the ones who sought to live life in our terms and we only knew whatever life we could carve out for ourselves; and we are the ones who God has called to know *Christ's Life alive in us!*

How can we know that and not be changed? How can we know that and not have it impact and change all of our relationships? We ought to be launched into whatever mission God has for us knowing that we are being empowered with the Spirit's engines!

Christ's Life gives us an abundance of the life we need for life!

In the Greek, the ζωv[4], or "life," that Jesus speaks of in John 10:10, the "abundant life," is the same "life" the apostle Paul describes in his epistles when he is speaking of *the new life* that we now have *in Christ*. It is dramatically contrasted to the former life that we had apart from Christ to the Life that we now have in him. The result of this contrast is so dramatic that Paul expresses it as our being, *"new creations in Christ."* "Therefore, if anyone is in Christ, he is a new creation; the old has gone, the new has come!" (2nd Corinthians 5:17)

God gives us his *Life* as he is birthing *spiritual life* in us when we are born again. And this is as distinctly a work of God as Adam's original creation. As the "Last Adam," Jesus gives us *Life* that is *eternal life*, life that is literally, *"Life-giving."* "So it is written, 'The first man Adam became a living being,' the last Adam, a 'life-giving spirit'" (1st Corinthians 15:45).

It is *new life* because *God's life* is now abiding in us, changing us from the inside and making us *"new creations in Christ Jesus"* that now defines how we are to relate to one another. As Paul says, "So from now on we regard no one from a worldly point of view. Though we once regarded Christ in this way, we do so no longer. Therefore, if anyone is in Christ,

---

[4]   ζωv, definition from BibleWorks 6, copy write 2003.

he is a *new creation*: the old has gone, *the new has come!* (2nd Corinthians 5:16-17)

This *"life-giving Spirit"* is at work in us now! Jesus has prayed that this work continue in all believers: "May they be brought to complete unity to let the world know that you sent me and have loved them even as you have loved me" (John 17:23).

Are we seeking God that this might be happening right now in our relationships with others? Are we asking him to manifest this part of *the Spirit's DNA* in us? It is part of *the redemptive DNA* that is ours in Christ, so let's ask him to bring this part of *his Life* alive in us!

The Spirit of God builds his ministry by the new life we share together!

Paul says that *God's Spirit* is at work in us individually, "Don't you know that you yourselves are God's temple and that God's Spirit lives in you" (1st Corinthians 3:16)? But God is not building his work in us as individuals so that we just individually know his presence. God is building his ministry in us so that we function together as the Body of Christ, a temple in which he has come to abide and make his presence known so that others see his Spirit's work in us and come to know him. He is building a spiritual temple made out of believers who he is calling from around the world!

We are not called to be Lone Rangers. As Peter says, "As you have come to Him, the Living Stone—rejected by men but chosen by God and precious to Him-you also, like living stones, are being built into a spiritual house" (1 Peter 2:4-5).

Paul puts it this way, "Consequently, you are no longer foreigners and aliens, but fellow citizens with God's people and members of God's household, built on the foundation of the apostles and prophets, with Christ Jesus himself as the chief cornerstone. In him the whole building is joined together and rises to become a *holy temple*, in the Lord. And in him you too are being built together to become a dwelling in which *God lives by His Spirit*" (Ephesians 2:19-21, emphasis mine)!

Why not ask, right now, even as I pause while I am writing, and ask God to restore this vital part of *his redemptive DNA* in our relationships with Him and others. "Lord, I have been estranged long enough from the kind of personal relationships that you have created me to enjoy. I know that my sin has separated me from you and others. Please forgive me on the basis of Christ's death and apply the benefits of his shed blood to me. Empower me with the mighty power of his resurrected life. Pour out your *Holy Spirit* in my life and in every relationship that I have. Enable grace to reign even over those relationships that have been strained and suffered from alienation in the past. Make my life an example of what it means to experience *the redemptive DNA* of *your Spirit's work in my life* so that I may now experience *new life* in my relationship with you and others. In Jesus' name I pray. Amen."

Consider how God is calling you to a "New Life Together" with the Body

1. Read Romans 6:4 and think about how comprehensive our *"new Life"* in Christ is? What areas of your life do you need to see *God's New Life* at work? Will you accept the challenge to pray every morning for God to touch that area of your life this week?

2. God gives *New Life* to all believers because *his Spirit* is within them. How does *God's New Life* need to impact your relationships? What relationship do you have right now where you sense the encouragement of *God's Spirit* every time you have fellowship with that person? What relationship do you have that is really difficult? How can you be an encouragement to the other person in this relationship so that they sense *God's New Life* at work in you? What relationship do you need to see *the Life* that only the blood of Jesus' can restore?

3. In heaven all believers are going to be living together
   for eternity! That might be scary if you are having a hard
   time with some people now! Will you ask God to bring
   His peace and grace to this relationship so that you
   can start experiencing a taste of heaven in the way
   you relate to them? Get a head start on glory now!

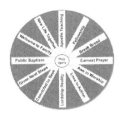

Chapter 7
God's DNA: Apostles' teaching

There ought to be no doubt that having Biblical teaching is a critical part of God's DNA of life for any healthy ministry. You can't grow further than the theology that you embrace. And the church birthed at Pentecost had the opportunity to sit at the feet of those who sat at the feet of Jesus. What an awesome privilege this would have been.

But there is a basic flaw in most of our thinking when we consider what this must have been like. When we read a phrase like what is recorded for us here by Luke, "apostles' teaching," the tendency is for us to let our 21st century computer Bible program brain click to the default mode and want to pull up for reference, "Brown Driver Briggs Hebrew Lexicon, Thayer Greek Lexicon, Gesenius-Hebrew Grammar, Burton's Moods and Tenses, Matthew Henry Commentaries, Spurgeon's Metropolitan Tabernacle Sermon Series (to see if Spurgeon preached on it!), Naves Topical Dictionary, Strong's Concordance, and our own Study Bible (that might be anything from the Spirit-Filled Study Bible to the Spirit of the Reformation Study Bible)."

And then we would pull out all the notes and syllabus notebooks from seminars that we have attended because we remember that some speaker said something somewhere about what we are studying. We might even get out the latest DVD's we had ordered on line, such as my friend, Dr.

Richard Pratt, Jr. latest series, "Building Systematic Theology." He probably would have covered some truth from God's Word that would help you in your study. It really would!

Truth is not true because of how we articulate it . . . but because it is true!

None of these Bible tools were present in the life of the early church. And it is important to bear in mind that the Holy Spirit had no trouble teaching the early church through the "limited" resource of sitting at the feet of the apostles! And the same is true today. God doesn't need our theological expertise to teach his people. He doesn't need us at all. He has chosen to use us in the process of declaring his truth to others; but it is not our refined abilities that make the message effective. It is the Spirit working in the hearts of men. We see that happening at Pentecost as the Spirit came upon the church (Acts 2:42).

My point is that we forget how uncomplicated the way Jesus taught really was. It revealed the most profound truths that had ever entered into the hearing of men, but the manner in which it was conveyed to them was simple. It was not sophisticated in the way we think it might have been. It was delivered by Jesus in sandaled feet. He spoke in parables. He taught stories to illustrate what knowing God was like inviting men to respond as they listened.

Jesus declared who God is and what he has done in creation and in spiritual rescue operations throughout history. And he did this in a way that declared the most profound truths through stories.

Later his disciples would do the same thing. Those who sat at Jesus' feet where now having others sit at their feet. Fishermen who had spent their lives at sea dealing with storms and falling fish prices told their stories. That's why John says, "Jesus did many other miraculous signs in the presence of his disciples, which are not recorded in this book. But these are written that you may believe that Jesus is the Christ, the Son of God, and that by believing you may have life in his name" (John 20:30-31).

John wrote about what he had seen while spending time walking with Jesus. And now he was inviting others to walk with him too by the stories he conveyed. "That which was from the beginning, which we have heard, which we have seen with our eyes, which we have looked at and our hands have touched—this we proclaim concerning the Word of Life. The Life appeared; we have seen it and testify to it, and we proclaim to you the eternal life, which was with the Father and has appeared to us. We proclaim to you what we have seen and heard, so that you also may have fellowship with us. And our fellowship is with the Father and with his Son, Jesus Christ" (1 John 1:1-3).

Truth isn't true because of who shares it . . . but because of God who has spoken it!

Paul was another man who had met Jesus. It was on a road to Damascus. It was a busy and dusty road but it became a road of rest and deliverance. Paul, who had formerly been a persecutor of the church, wrote about his stories.

He wrote stories of his rescue (Galatians 1:4; 2nd Timothy 4:18). He wrote stories of his hardships (2nd Corinthians 6:3-10). He wrote stories of his being abandoned and of his being attacked (2nd Timothy 4:9, 14). He wrote stories of his being at the end of himself unable to go on (2nd Corinthians 1:8). He wrote stores about his unanswered prayer being answered by grace (2nd Corinthians 12:7-10). He wrote stories about his tears (Philippians 3:18). He wrote stories about his triumphs (1st Corinthians 15:56).

His stories where so unpretentious that some thought he was too naïve to be heard. Paul responded by saying, "But I do not think I am in the least inferior to those 'super-apostles.' I may not be a trained speaker, but I do have knowledge. We have made this perfectly clear to you in every way"

(2nd Corinthians 11: 5-6). And yet some still persisted in their arrogance and they missed the blessing of sitting at his feet and hearing his story, his God-story.

There were those as the church at Corinth who would rather be exploited than just hear the simple truth from Paul. "In fact, you even put up with anyone who enslaves you or exploits you or takes advantage of you or pushes himself forward or slaps you in the face. To my shame I admit that we were too weak for that!" (2nd Corinthians 11:19-21)

Have we become so sophisticated that we can't hear stories anymore?

People get side-tracked with the wrong things. It seems to be in our natural dna to do so. We don't see the incredible truths that God gives us through his stories. We just look at them and decide if they are "appropriate" for our use. And if we decide that they aren't going to be of any benefit to us, we set them aside like a pair of old shoes that we wouldn't want to be seen in public wearing. Do we think that we have become too sophisticated to hear God stories anymore?

What we forget is that it is about Jesus and not about the ones he chooses to use in our lives. If it were about the messengers, they would tell their own stories in such a way that they would make the story about them. But it is never about them. It is about Jesus and what he is continuing to do in writing new stories in people's lives.

Who told their story to you?

It is his story, the Jesus Life story that is perhaps most clearly told when it is told by those who seem to be the most unlikely ones he would have ever chosen to tell his story. Yet that's when we know God is telling the story through them.

As Paul put it, "But God chose the foolish things of the world to shame the wise; God chose the weak things of the world to shame the strong. He chose the lowly things of this world and the despised things-and the things that are not-to nullify the things that are, so that no one may boast before him. It is because of him that you are in Christ Jesus, who has become for us wisdom from God-that is our righteousness, holiness and redemption. Therefore, as it is written: 'Let him who boasts boast in the Lord.'" (1st Corinthians 1:27-31)

Those were the story tellers who were telling their story, their Jesus story, to those sitting at their feet following Pentecost. And that's the kind of story tellers we still need. We need those who will tell their Jesus story.

Truth told in Stories helps us on our Life Journeys

We have this *apostles teaching DNA* present in the early church (Acts 2:42). They shared the truth they had learned about Jesus. But this included how this truth came to be expressed on their journey with him. Truth was found by them to be true. And they shared why. They never saw truth as abstract theological concept. They saw it as life because it is found in Jesus who said, "I am the way, the truth, and the life" (John 14:6).

It is absolute for it came from the mouth of him who lives forever. But it is more than just words that can be studied. It has live giving power as Paul said, "I am not ashamed of the gospel, because it is the power of God" (Romans 1:16). The author of Hebrews makes the same point, "For the word of God is *living* and *active*. Sharper than any double-edged sword, it penetrates even to the dividing soul and spirit, joints and marrow; it judges the thoughts and attitudes of the heart" (Hebrews 4:12). It is *God's DNA* because it is *"living and active"* in our very souls!

Studying the Bible isn't enough unless you find Jesus in the Story!

Jesus rebuked the Pharisees because all they were doing was studying the Scriptures and forgetting that the One they spoke about was standing before them. "You diligently study the Scriptures because you think that by them you possess eternal life. These are the Scriptures that testify about me. Yet you refuse to come to me to have life" (John 5:39-40).

We can study all our lives and have use of the best Bible tools available in the history of the church and still miss Jesus. Jesus isn't isolated theological articulation. Jesus is the way, the truth, and the life (John 14:6).

Jesus is truth incarnate! Jesus was never isolated from life. He is life. And in his life he showed us the way by declaring the truth to us. But he did this in stories.

Jesus wasn't the only one that made truth real. Jeremiah served in a time of alienation and exile from God because of real sins. He wasn't concerned to make things complicated. He said, "Furthermore, tell the people, 'This is what the LORD says: See, I am setting before you the way of life and the way of death" (Jeremiah 21:8). There it is. There is the way to death apart from God. And there is the way of life in God. Choose your way. Such a decision comes with clarity in a generation that demands sophistication or it is not seen to be appropriately presented.

Stories help us keep our feet on the path that Jesus walks on.

There is nothing more relevant to our journeys than the roads we are taking. It is Jesus who invites us on a journey in him. He is "the way, the truth, and the life." He invites is to take the right road. He bids us follow him.

Our problem is that we want to define everything before we set out on our journeys. It is too risky for us to just trust Jesus as though he knows the way. We have to see it all worked out. We have to have our 3 yr. plan, our 5 yr. plan, and our life plan. If we speak to someone who doesn't, we cannot believe that they have anything to offer us. Why it would be like sitting on a dusty floor with Paul!

So we study things. Then we study them some more. We get the latest insights on archeological digs and theological studies. We plan and organize with the latest ministry model and we see how every detail can be justified by our philosophy of ministry and our mission statements.

If we don't live our stories we try and put Jesus on the self!

The only thing is . . . that by the time we have gotten all of our books off the shelf, had all the time we needed in pursuit of doing things in the right way, and then determine by committee who is spiritual enough to join us in achieving our new found plan . . . we find that Jesus has gone. You see he never stopped walking along the path because he remained "the way" even though we couldn't trust him to be.

He had waited for a while you know. He has stopped hoping that we would soon come out of our planning meetings and follow him. But we never came, so he left. He went further down the trail to where others were, simpler than us, more unsophisticated, and too naïve . . . they simply trusted and followed him. And the thing is . . . they are the ones who are smiling and singing and appear to be worshipping Jesus in a way we have never known. Curious indeed!

You see you can't put Jesus on the self and ask that he wait until you are ready to take him down and read more about him, study him, and then put him back besides your other treasured books. You can't control him like that because he is not only the "way" and the "truth" but he is also the "life" and he will get off the shelf and walk!

Jesus shows us how the Bible comes alive with life stories!

If you really have "believed" Jesus came to give us life abundant, you would do more than expect a theological argument. You would expect Life! And that is what you get in Jesus. His Spirit beings *God's DNA, his Life* to us.

We have the tendency to hit the default button by thinking we can think our way though our Christian lives. We can do that. We really don't need Jesus to do that. We can do that on our own. But we can also miss *life* while we are thinking about living! If we come to the place where we think we can figure out our lives, it really only means that we are yet to enter God's classroom of Life.

But God has a way of making sure that we don't miss this class! And when we start taking it, it will not be enough for us that we "know" something about what the Bible has to say about this or that. We are going to find ourselves seeking out others who have gone though similar challenges and ask them, "How did you handle this?" "What did you do?" "How did you keep your faith through this trial?" "How did you apply this truth of Scriptures to your circumstances?"

The point being, we are going to want to walk with someone who has been on the same journey. It is not going to be enough that we know someone who "lectures" on this subject. We are going to want to know the believer who has tragically lost his wife, or whose son has lived with a disease most of his life, or whose daughter was taken by knife point and held hostage and robbed. We are going to want to have someone like Paul commends that can, "comfort us" with the comfort they have themselves received from God (2nd Corinthians 1:3-7).

We are going to want to know the guy who was kicked out of a church but who is more in love with Jesus than ever. We are going to want to know his wife who stayed with her man when no one else but God did! We aren't going to care too hoots about just getting out a syllabus from a seminar we had taken. If fact we are going to test what we were taught at those seminars to see if they are true.

God has a way of correcting bad theology with life!

I tell people that God has a way of correcting bad theology with life. For example, if you were taught that believers never get sick and you get sick, you are going to start believing that what you believed must me wrong! Then, if you are blessed, God will bring someone into your life who has had many life struggles and who has discovered that Jesus said that this was normal for those who believe. Jesus said, "I have told you these things, so that in me you may have peace. In this world you will have trouble. But take heart! I have overcome the world" (John 16:33). Your experience in life is going to correct your bad theology because it is going to put you in a position to hear, really hear, what Jesus has to say.

By being around others who have journeyed in Jesus, more than you have, you are going to discover that the Bible really is alive with truth that is relevant to your life. You are also going to see that the truth proclaimed in the Bible, will come to be expressed in the life journeys of his people.

The reason is simple. God's Spirit will be working to bring what is true, as found in the Bible, to be true in the lives of God's people because they have come to know Him who is the truth and their lives are being transformed in conformity to that which has set them free! And suddenly, truth is going to make sense.

The Bible actually teaches that we are living in a broken and fallen world and that you will suffer if for no other reason than because you are still alive in that world (Genesis 3:17-19; Romans 5:12). Pretty soon you realize that there are all kinds of reasons why you may be suffering and none of them have to do with how spiritual you are (Romans 8:22). You may in fact suffer because you are spiritual (2nd Corinthians 12:8)! But the presence of suffering does not mean the absence of God or your faith in him. It might actually show the complete opposite that God really is with you and that you really have faith in him! Job is the example par excel lance (Job 1:8)!

Struggles in Life are Opportunities for the Life of Jesus to be seen!

When you find yourself in a struggle for life you are going to want to know someone who knows something about life! You aren't going to be searching for that article you once read entitled, "Christian Theology and Cultural Tendencies in the 21st Century." If you do get something out of that article, then you are going to know that Jesus really has come because no one has ever been helped from an article like that unless Jesus came!

We still seem to think that the only way someone learns is through doctrinal classes, or seminars, or through Sunday school classes, or through gifted preachers that articulate truth in packaged sermons.

We can learn some tremendous truths from these things, but they won't stick unless they get hammered out on the anvils of our personal life struggles. They will quickly become something we "remember" studying. We may be able to quote a turn of phrase that we thought insightful. But we won't remember much more! But they won't become something we are living . . . at least not unless we come to see our need for them and check them out once more!

We need to see how important it is to learn from others who have sat at Jesus' feet. We need to be like those first disciples who could have sat and listened to Paul or Peter or Luke because they knew that they were getting truth from those who had been with Jesus.

We need Jesus to raise up his journeymen and journeywomen who can share with us how Jesus has led them all the way in all of life's struggles and victories.

"They devoted themselves to the apostles' teaching"

It is important to see that New Testament believers were learning this way. They heard Jesus speak in synagogues once in a while, but his messages were very short and often asked more questions of others than giving any answers himself! Jesus taught in life relationships because that is how truth is manifested. He said, "Come follow me," and in the context of their journey with him they were changed.

In the Book of Acts, we read about believers on a journey with others who had traveled with him. When the Bible says, "They devoted themselves to the apostles' teaching," it means that they really were devoting themselves to the teaching that was literally coming from the mouths of the apostles or from the mouths of those who had been taught by the apostles. So what they were hearing was coming to them from those who had learned "truth in life." And that is what I think God always intended for His people to do; to learn truth in the context of life, so that we really learn.

Parents share their Jesus Journey with their children!

We can see this in the Old Testament by looking at just two examples of how God said people should be taught. In the first place we see God's instruction as to "how" fathers were to teach their children. "Hear, O Israel: The Lord our God, the Lord is one. Love the Lord your God with all your heart and with all your soul and with all your strength. These commands that I give you today are to be upon your hearts. Impress them on your children.

"Talk about them when you sit at home and when you walk along the road, when you lie down and when you get up. Tie them as symbols on your hands and bind them on your foreheads. Write them on the doorframes of your houses and on your gates . . ." In the future, when your son asks you, 'What is the meaning of the stipulations, decrees and laws the Lord our God has commanded you?' Tell him: 'We were slaves of Pharaoh in Egypt, but the Lord brought us out of Egypt with a mighty hand. Before our eyes the Lord sent miraculous signs and wonders-great and terrible-upon Egypt and Pharaoh and his whole household. But he brought us out from there to bring us in and give us the land promised on oath to our forefathers. The Lord commanded us to obey all these decrees and to fear the Lord our God, so that we might always prosper and be kept alive, as is the case today'" (Deuteronomy 6:4-9, 20-24).

I must make a couple of critical points here. First of all there is no way that you can say that the theology that is being conveyed is simplistic or naïve. At a quick glance anyone can see a theology of the Godhead being developed ("Hear O Israel: The Lord our God, the Lord is one"), a theology of redemption ("We were slaves of Pharaoh in Egypt, but the Lord brought us out of Egypt with a mighty hand"), and a practical theology ("The Lord commanded us to obey . . . that it might go well for us") that was to flow from the points made regarding "who" God is and "what" God had done through the redemption of his people from Egypt.

But what we do see is deep theology being simply taught. Children were taught as they sat at the feet of their dads, as they walked along the trails of life and as they reflected at the day's end as they laid down to rest.

They were being discipled. But it wasn't a class room situation where material was studied, lectured on in class, tested on at the end of the semester, and grades given to be posted on their parent's tent! No. The children were to be discipled in life, by being taught the truth in the context of their life journey with their parents and the community of the brethren, the whole of Israel. Their disciplers were their parents. And they taught them at every life opportunity as they sat, they walked, and they traveled with God and each other.

Solomon shared his life journey with his son

There is another obvious example. It flows from the life of Solomon and his desire to pass on "wisdom" to his son. Proverbs is one of the coolest and most overlooked books in the Bible. It teaches us so much about what true discipleship is. We are to be sharing truth in the context of sharing our lives. When we do that we convey wisdom from God for we do more than just "tell" people what ought to be believed, we explain to them why it is practical, and we show them how to apply it in their lives.

One such example is Solomon's warning to his son, "My son, keep my commands and do not forsake your mother's teaching. Bind them upon your heart forever; fasten them around your neck" (Proverbs 6:20). Notice how similar this language is to what we previously saw with fathers teaching their children. This pattern of practical life-truth-journey instruction was continuing from Moses to Solomon as the means of discipling the next generation.

And to show how relevant it was, Solomon warned his son about the adulterous woman. "For these commands are a lamp, this teaching a light, and the corrections of discipline are the way of life, keeping you from the immoral woman, from the smooth tongue of the wayward wife. Do not lust in your heart after her beauty or let her captivate you with her eyes, for the prostitute reduces you to a loaf of bread, and the adulteress preys upon your very life" (Proverbs 6:23-25).

In both of these examples, whether under Moses or Solomon, *practical theology* was paramount to *godly discipleship*. But the problem is that when we even hear the word "discipleship," we conjure up images of sitting in classes, making discipleship appointments, and attending seminars. All of those things can be incredibly fruitful in the process of discipleship; but they do not reflect the core essence of discipleship which rest in *the ministry of the Spirit* using *the Word of God* in our lives.

Apostles shared their life journey

What is at *the core DNA* of the discipleship that we see in Acts is found in the phrase, *"apostles' teaching."* This phrase conveys both elements critical for discipleship and health in the Body of Christ: Teaching, yes. But teaching being taught by those who have themselves discovered the truth of what is being taught, and seen the benefit of applying it to their lives, as well as having, in their weaknesses and sins, had to overcome their failures from not doing so; while discovering the grace and love of God through their journey which is powerful enough, through the Holy Spirit's presence in them, to bring victory out of defeat.

We see this exhibited out of Paul's life and ministry when he said, "As apostles of Christ we could have been a burden to you, but we were gentle among you, like a mother caring for her little children. We loved you so much that we were delighted to share with you not only the gospel of God but our lives as well, because you had become so dear to us" (1st Thessalonians 2:6-8).

So be very careful about looking for *theological articulation* without *life application*. We don't want to be applying our 21st century point of view, a collective-researched-documented-historically developed-theologically defined point of view that those literally sitting at the apostles' feet would not have heard. We don't want to read back into the Acts 2 what we have come to expect today. Instead, may God be gracious to bring the blessings of what was present in Acts 2 to us in today!

We are also called to share our life journey in Jesus!

I would argue that we actually ought to allow *the Holy Spirit* to shape our lives by what was the Biblical pattern for discipleship which was not only teaching truth, but teaching truth in life circumstances. And to be honest this requires more discipline that just teaching theological information.

You have to not only know what the Bible is teaching, but you have to pray that God will enable you by his Spirit to present it in a way that will communicate best to those who are hearing the message. That's discipleship! And that's what was happening in Acts 2 as believers sat at the apostles' feet.

Jesus said, "For I did not speak of my own accord, but the Father who sent me commanded me *what* to say and *how* to say it" (John 12:49). And if that is the pattern for how even Jesus learned ministry from the Father, if that is the pattern of how Jesus taught ministry to His disciples, if that is the pattern we see happening in Acts, don't you think that we need to start following the Bible's pattern for ministry?

God-Theology is not just lectured, it is lived. Not abstract truth, but truth on fire! As Jeremiah cried out, "His word is in my heart like a fire, a fire shut up in my bones. I am weary of holding it in; indeed I cannot!" (Jeremiah 20:9)

God's Life and Truth came to us in Jesus. Jesus said, "I am the way, the truth, and the life" (John 14:6). If the truth in Jesus is going to reach people, we have to use the way of Jesus by sharing truth in the context of life. Otherwise no one will want to seek him because they will not have seen his life in us![5]

Remember, our 21st Century approach can easily hit the default button in ministry. It might be helpful to know that not even "The Apostles' Creed" had been formulated by the end of their lives! It was something they believed and it reflects the truths they taught, but it wasn't formulated by them.

Early church fathers shared their life journey

We know that as John the apostle sat at the feet of Jesus, Polycarp sat at John's feet and Irenaeus sat at the feet of Polycarp. We are not without witness or testimony as to what the apostles taught or believed. The New Testament is itself the record of the Apostolic Teaching, but "the apostles'

---

[5]   Eugene H. Peterson, THE JESUS WAY (Grand Rapids: Eerdmans, 2007) is perhaps the most insightful book written in this area.

teaching" wasn't formulated as it has been over the centuries into systematic theology, historical theology, and biblical theology (not that the other 'theologies' aren't biblical, but this is a name for a particular discipline in approaching theology study).

It was simply truth taught by the apostles through the stories and parables and sayings of Jesus that they had heard, or witnessed, or confirmed as authenticate. And it would have included their journey's experience and how the truth of the gospel was being worked out in their lives as the Holy Spirit continued to teach them.

It is important for us to understand this so that we don't read back into the Acts 2 account that early believers were sitting at the apostles' feet and hearing, "An encyclopedia of theological articles dealing with the dynamics in addressing a Roman cultural in decline with the witness of 1st century revelation!"

We might want to do that, though it doesn't sound very inviting! But what we must also not fail to see is that the apostles were conveying the truth of Scripture. It would have included what Jesus taught and what they had learned along their journey's with him. But maybe to our surprise, it would also have included a comprehensive view of redemptive history.

After he was raised from the dead, Jesus said to his disciples, "This is what I told you while I was still with you: Everything must be fulfilled that is written in the Law of Moses, the Prophets and the Psalms.' Then he opened their minds so they could understand the Scriptures. He told them, 'This is what is written: The Christ will suffer and rise from the dead on the third day, and repentance and forgiveness of sins will be preached in his name to all nations, beginning at Jerusalem. You are witnesses of these things. I am going to send you what my Father promised; but stay in the city until you have been clothed with power from on high'" (Luke 24:44-49).

The apostles had stayed and they had been empowered with the Holy Spirit from on high! And they would have passed on to the early church what Jesus had opened their minds to understand.

Our life journey has become part of the story as well!

The apostles had been taught by Jesus himself, they had been empowered by the Spirit of God, and they were now seeing the church birthed and sitting at their feet so that they could pass on to the next generation of believers what God had taught them!

What classes those must have been! The best teachers in the world who had personally been taught by the Teacher were now teaching new believers, seeing God open their hearts to understand, as well, all that was taught in the Scriptures regarding Jesus!

What the apostles taught was a core DNA element in the early church and it continues to be so wherever the Holy Spirit is working today. The early church would not have had access to the wealth of theological reflection which 2000 years of the Holy Spirit's teaching of the church; but their learning would not have been diminished because they were taught first hand by those who walked in sandaled feet with the Messiah.

As John the apostle wrote, "That which was from the beginning, which we have heard, which we have seen with our eyes, which we have looked at and our hands have touched-this we proclaim concerning the Word of life" (1 John 1:1).

This is a far cry from the approach used where "truth" is taught apart from "life." There was nothing abstract about what the apostles' believed. It was learned and taught in the context of life. John's own testimony says, "This we proclaim concerning the Word of life" (1 John 1:1). Christ is the Incarnate Truth. He is God in the flesh. And He lived out, fleshed out, who God is and what it meant to enter into a relationship with Him.

Truth communicated a vibrant relationship with the living God. There was nothing dispassionate by what the apostles believed. If we only have a growing wealth of knowledge, if what we believe is only articulated and packaged without the vibrant *Life of Christ* being seen, it is not Christianity. It may reflect the truth of what is taught in the Bible, but Christianity brings Christ to people!

John the Baptist prepared the way for the coming of Jesus and he said of Jesus' ministry, "But one more powerful than I will come, the thongs of whose sandals I am not worthy to untie. He will baptize you with the Holy Spirit and with fire" (Luke 3:16).

That fire fell at Pentecost! "When the day of Pentecost came, they were together in one place. Suddenly a sound like a blowing of a violent wind came from heaven and filled the whole house where they were sitting. They saw what seemed to be tongues of fire that separated and came to rest on each of them" (Acts 2:1-3).

Christ had come, as John the Baptist said He would, and baptized His people with fire. And what do we see happening except Peter, who had formerly in fear denied Jesus three times, rising to stand before thousands to proclaim the Lord Christ with preaching that could only be characterized as being on fire!

The point being that the early church did not just receive theological formulations, most of which were not developed until centuries later. But what they did receive was *truth on fire!* They had been baptized with not only *the Spirit* but with *fire* and their lives showed it (Luke 3:16; Acts 2:4).

God's Spirit had brought the presence of God into their lives and you can't have him without being changed (2nd Corinthians 3:16-18)! We see this because truth now was being spoken by the mouths of those who were willing to give their lives to defend what they had come to believe and live. And because God's *fire* had come into their lives they became his *fire starters* across the Roman Empire and beyond.

It is also a *Life theology* also because the Spirit brings Christ's life to us. Believers become living epistles that have to find their voice to bear witness of the grace life they have received in Christ (2nd Corinthians 3:2). Other people can see that their lives have changed because they actually have! They are no longer who they were though they still aren't all that they are becoming.

So even their studying of the letters that the apostles had written was no mere exercise in what they needed to study! It was an encounter with the living God! And because the Spirit of God is moving, truth is being proclaimed and lived reflecting *God's DNA! God's life* in us will manifest *his truth on fire* as Jeremiah said, "His word is in my heart like a fire, a fire shut up in my bones. I am weary of holding it in; indeed, I cannot" (Jeremiah 20:9).

If we aren't experiencing this, maybe we better start looking at the "way" we minister in our churches. Maybe we actually ought to go back to the Bible's pattern of discipleship and see that the apostles' doctrine was taught by the apostles who lived lives set aflame for Christ and ask God to kindle our hearts with His truth again!

Consider how "the Apostles' Teaching" impacts your life:

1. Who do you see as someone who is mentoring you in the faith? It may be a believer that you have looked up to for a long time or a new friend; it may be a church

member or a Christian neighbor. But who is it that you really share your heart with?

2. Think about what area in your life that you struggle the most with. Ask your mentor to help you discover some truths from the Bible that would directly speak to this need in your life. But for now, what would that area of need be?

3. Now let's look at this from another angle. Since you have given your life to Christ you have God's Holy Spirit in your life. He is empowering you to overcome things that you had no idea you would ever be free from; sins that had formerly been your master (Romans 6:15-18).

   The Holy Spirit is also going to use you to encourage someone else because of what you have learned on your journey (2nd Corinthians 1:3-4). He has given you spiritual gifts to help make that happen (1st Corinthians 12:7). With that in mind you need to know that God is fashioning you to be used in the lives of others just like God has used others to encourage you.

   Question: Who has God put in your life that you can use the insights that you have learned along the trail with your journey in Jesus to be an encouragement to them? What's their name? Start praying for opportunities to minister to them.

4. Consider meeting with the person that God has placed on your heart to encourage this week. What are you studying in God's Word that might be an encouragement to them? Write down your daily insights from your times with Jesus this week so that you can share them with the person God has put on your heart to mentor.

5. Remember: Discipleship is sharing not only the truth of God's word, but your life so that others can see the

reality of God's word visible in you. We are all living epistles. We proclaim a message each day with our lives. Read 2nd Corinthians 3:3 and spend time in prayer thanking God for the changes His Spirit is bringing into your life.

6. The classic passage that speaks to the Bible as being the inspired Word of God is 2nd Timothy 3:16-17. Read that passage and note why God has given us that inspired Word, why he has "breathed life" into it . . .

   a. See if it isn't for helping us on our journeys . . . list the ways it does that

   b. See if there is any hint at all of Paul suggesting that God has given us his Word for simply educational purposes. Isn't it for edification and correction, and for helping us on our Jesus journey?

7. For help in Studying and Living on your journey in Jesus:

   Dr. Richard Pratt at Third Millennium Ministries www.thirdmill.org

   Dr. Pat Morley at Man in the Mirror www.maninthemirror.org

   This We Believe, by John K. Akers, John Woodbridge, Kevin Harney, Mass Market Paperback (Feb. 2001)

   An excellent Women's Ministry resource is www.christianwomentoday.com

   Also for a general reference see www.bible.org

Chapter 8
God's DNA: Fellowship

I have never met a Christian who didn't think that fellowship was important. It is perhaps the number one thing that draws people to a particular ministry or keeps them from joining if they sense that they can't get very good fellowship from that church. So everyone is looking for it. Church leaders want to make sure that they have it in their churches because they want to grow. And Church members stay or leave based upon whether they feel their spiritual needs are being met through the fellowship that they are receiving in their church.

The thing is we can't create fellowship. We can simulate it by making sure certain "things" are part of any ministry; such as having a "fellowship time" where believers can "mingle" following the worship service; or having "fellowship groups" where believers meet in small group settings in members' homes. But having the provision for fellowship in the church is not the same thing as actually having fellowship because fellowship isn't something we can produce.

Fellowship is actually a "gift" from God. It is part of the manifestation of *God's DNA* because it reflects a person's having come into *fellowship* with God which provides the basis for *fellowship* with other Christians. First a person is reconciled to God by placing faith in the Lord Jesus Christ whose shed blood is accepted by God as the payment for their sin. This happens through the ministry of the Holy Spirit applying the work of Christ to our lives. "He saved us, not because of righteous things we had done, but because of his mercy. He saved us through the washing of rebirth and renewal by the Holy Spirit, whom he poured out on us generously through Jesus Christ our Savior." (Titus 3:5-6)

How do you enter into the Fellowship Reality?

When we are forgiven by God, we enter into a *fellowship reality* because there is nothing to separate us from God since our sin has been removed. David said, "As far as the east is from the west, so far has he removed our transgressions from us" (Psalm 103:12).

One of the fruits of that fellowship with God is our having fellowship with other believers. Since all of God's children have experienced the removal of their sin, there is nothing to separate us from each another. That is as long as we continue to walk in the light of belonging to God and being united to one another through Jesus. "But if we walk in the light, as he is the light, we have fellowship with one another, and the blood of Jesus, his Son, purifies us from all sin" (1 John 1:7).

That's why we must keep sin out of our relationships. As surely as sin separates us from having fellowship with God, it will also become a wedge to drive separation among believers so that they are prevented from having fellowship with one another. The Bible teaches us about the importance of keeping accounts short by forgiving one another as God in Christ has forgiven us. "Bear with each other and forgive whatever grievances you may have against one another. Forgive as the Lord forgave you" (Colossians 3:13).

If we fail to do this, the loss of fellowship will be immediate because it will impact all of our relationships. Our sin against God impacts relationships here on earth. David said his sin with Bathsheba was primarily a sin against God. "Against you, you only have I sinned and done what is evil in your sight" (Psalm 51:4). There were obvious consequences in David's other relationships, but David emphasized that these consequences were exactly that; consequences not originating causes.

On the other hand, if we have sinned against our neighbor this will impact our relationship with God in heaven. Jesus said, "Therefore, if you are offering your gift at the altar and there remember that your brother has something against you, leave your gift there in front of the altar. First go and be reconciled to your brother; then come and offer your gift" (Matthew 5:23-24). Don't pretend that you can treat others with contempt and then worship God as though nothing has happened.

Death comes into our relationships when we sin against our neighbor or against our God because death is a consequence to sin. This is in stark contrast to the life God wants us to experience because of Jesus. John said, "The Life appeared; we have seen it and testify to it, and we proclaim to you what we have seen and heard, so that you also may have fellowship with us. And our fellowship is with the Father and with His Son, Jesus Christ" (1 John 1:2-3).

Fellowship comes from being in relationship with God through Jesus

It is important for us to remember that we have fellowship with others only in so far as we have come to have fellowship with God. This is where most churches have gotten things backward. They think that they have "fellowship" with other Christians because we like them, or because we agree with them, or because they worship the way we do, or teach the Bible the way we are used to having it taught. But fellowship is not derived from anything inherent within us or present because there are similarities between us and others.

Fellowship exists among the brethren because all of those present are walking with God and one another through the cleansing power of forgiveness that the Holy Spirit has applied to their personal lives and relationships together. Fellowship comes first with God then others.

We have fellowship with other believers having been united to Christ. We aren't united with each other apart from Christ. We may like each other or enjoy certain things together. But as soon as disagreements arise, whatever surface kinship we may have felt will disappear as the morning midst!

So often over the years I have seen people trying to be united, trying to create fellowship by insisting certain things like everyone being involved in this activity or that. But if you can't go, you are said to be missing fellowship. This is not biblical. We may have missed a meeting or a picnic but we haven't missed fellowship. Unless of course we have sinned in some way but if that is the case then going to a picnic would not have changed things!

Fellowship doesn't come from trying to pressurize everyone into the same mold. Fellowship comes from the union that is ours in Christ and as we walk with him we have fellowship with one another and the blood of Jesus will cleanse us in our journey together (1 John 1:7).

This is not how most Christians tend to think about fellowship, but it is the Biblical view and ought to become ours. And the sooner it does, the quicker we will experience true fellowship with one another because we will not be united because we happen to agree with each other about certain things or practices or even theology; but we will be united to each other because, as John puts it, "Our fellowship is with the Father and with His Son, Jesus Christ" (1 John 1:3).

Fellowship with anyone is possible when you have fellowship with God!

And we see this coming to expression at Pentecost as Jews from all over the Roman world had gathered at Jerusalem for the festival, and having been convicted by the gospel message, they surrendered their hearts and lives with Jesus, coming to have fellowship with Him where before they had been at enmity. Without anyone saying to them, "We hope you experience good fellowship here among us, please sign our visitor's welcome register so that we might make you feel welcome; we even have a pen and a mug with our church name on it that we want to give you for being new among us today."

Thank God that didn't happen! (Not that it isn't nice to get a new pen or coffee mug . . . I've picked up a few myself lately!) But what did happen, because they had been convicted, invited, and committed by being baptized and welcomed into the number of the redeemed, they experienced fellowship! They had come to have fellowship with God because they had come to know Him. And they came to have fellowship with one another because they had received God's Spirit which signified their being accepted into God's family.

John would later write, "How great is the love the Father has lavished on us, that we should be called children of God" (1 John 3:1). This happened as God's Spirit worked in their lives bringing them to faith in Christ. And having been united to Christ, by being born into the family of God, they had received God's Spirit to affirm that they belonged to Him. Paul wrote, "For you did not receive a spirit that makes you a slave again to fear, but you received the Spirit of sonship. And by Him we cry, 'Abba, Father'" (Romans 8:15).

God's Spirit brings this Fellowship DNA into our lives!

When God's Spirit comes into our lives, John says, "God's seed remains in him . . . because he has been born of God" (1 John 3:9). What an awesome thought this is, that God's seed, God's DNA, remains in us! That's why we have fellowship with our heavenly Father, and with His Son Jesus, who is not ashamed to call us His brothers! "Both the one who makes men holy and those who are made holy are of the same family. So Jesus is not ashamed to call them brothers. He says, 'I will declare your name to my brothers" (Hebrews 2:11-12).

I have been a pastor for over 30 years and I have never, in either America or in Australia, found two brothers or two sisters alike in every detail. The truth is that we are often so different that we drive each other crazy and wonder how they got to be part of the "family of God!" It's a good thing God doesn't consult us as to who should or shouldn't be part of His family; because if He consulted us, He would be obliged to consult other family members about us; and it may be "us" that "they" don't want in the family!

But God calls who He will to be part of His family. It is His Sovereign choice. We see this affirmed even at Pentecost. "And the Lord added to their number daily those who were being saved" (Acts 2:47; see also Acts 13:48). God called, God birthed, God anointed His children with His Spirit so that they would have fellowship with Him . . . and in the process . . . grow in grace and come to have fellowship with one another!

That can be the tuff part! But it can also be the part that causes us to grow the most. It forces us to consider just how different we all really are. And all of the weaknesses and sins that come out in the interaction between brothers and sisters forces us to see that God's grace are bigger than any of us! None of us would have a right to sit at the table unless God had been gracious to us! But He has . . . and He has been gracious to others too! And when you start to get that . . . you start to understand grace . . . and you start to experience fellowship with one another because you really do have fellowship with God!

The thing that gets me, really gets me, is that a lot of believers don't seem to understand this! I'm not trying to be cute or simplistic or naïve, but it really isn't that hard! When we are born again, we are born into God's family. This ought to overwhelm us at God's grace to us. We ought to be excited for anyone else who comes into God's family and becomes our brother or sister in Christ. But instead we treat other family members as though they don't belong. We don't like their perspectives on life or ministry. We don't like that they don't like the same hymns we like. We don't like the way they think.

We don't like what they want to do to change things in our church. We don't like them.

You really are my brother or sister in Christ, you really are!

But we are members one of another in Christ! We are in Jesus together. God is our heavenly Father. The Holy Spirit is our comforter and grace giver. God is in us and we are in Him. And the fact that we don't live like that stinks.

If anything is ever going to change, we are going to have to rediscover that *fellowship with God*, and through Christ *with one another*, is part of *God's DNA* for us as believers. It was a vibrant part of the believers in Acts who didn't mind even selling their own property in order that others in their new family are provided for. They were meeting daily to learn together and break bread together. They met in one another's home and showed hospitality to one another. And they did this without any program being forced upon them. They were not manipulated into believing they should love one another and care for one another. They just did. And they did so because of the life-giving *DNA of Fellowship* with God that was transforming their lives to value the life journeys of their brethren and join with them in their journey in Jesus together.

Consider how "Fellowship" has impacted your life

1. Have you ever met someone for the first time and felt like you had known them forever, only to find out that they were a Christian too? What you were experiencing reflected the unity that is ours in Christ! Why not pick up the phone and call that friend you have been meaning to call for a long time and let them know how grateful you are that God has brought them into your life!

2. One of the main concerns of this chapter is to show how believers often don't have fellowship with one

another because they have fallen out of fellowship with God. Make sure that you are keeping fellowship with Jesus. Take time to commune with your Heavenly Father each day through Him. Ask the Holy Spirit to help you in your prayers to be honest to God about what has kept you from praying more. Perhaps it is because you don't feel that God would be interested in your particular struggles. Perhaps you feel your problems seem to inconsequential to bother God with. Perhaps you are ashamed of things that you have done and don't know if God will hear you if you are really that honest with Him. But consider . . .

a. There is nothing God doesn't already know about you anyway! Psalm 139:1-4

b. And yet God made you for a special purpose! Psalm 139:13-16

c. So why not thank Him for what He is doing in your life and ask Him to encourage you on your journey in Jesus! Psalm 139:17-18; 143:8; 147:2, 3

Chapter 9
God's DNA: Break Bread

As baptism is to the new believer, so breaking bread is to those who are remaining on their journey in Jesus. Baptism signifies the start of a journey in Jesus. Breaking bread shows that believers are remaining on that journey. It is part of *God's DNA* that shows our union with Christ and our fellowship with the Body of Christ continues to be a reality for us. It was commanded by Christ just like baptism because of its importance in our participating in Christ's life in a visible way (Matthew 28:19; Luke 22:19).

That's why we see the church community breaking bread with each other from the start (Luke 22:19; Acts 2:42, 46; 20:7; 27:35; 1st Corinthians 10:16, 17; 11:26). And that's why it continues to be celebrated to this day. Where ever God is doing a work of grace in the lives of people, they will come to participate in this *DNA of the Christian community*.

Have we lost our way on our journey by not breaking bread together?

It seems, however, that "breaking bread" has lost its place as an important part of *God's DNA* in some church circles. At least when compared to other things. It seems that churches will do anything to assure that they have a good music ministry or youth program, yet sadly, there appears to be little emphasis on the need for the brethren to break bread together. In thinking about this it might be helpful to realize that there was no music ministry or youth program at Pentecost!

There weren't any bands playing to stir the crowd and create an "atmosphere of worship." There wasn't an organ playing in an earlier service to create the feeling of "reverence" either. No one wondered whether traditional hymns or contemporary ones were going to be played before Peter's message. And Peter didn't have to worry about making sure he said the same things in both services.

No keyboard, no organ, no worship team, but no choir either! No one got a bulletin when they walked in and no one signed a guest register or received an ink pen with the church logo on it for visiting on the day.

But what they did do was listen to Peter's preaching about their sin in participating in the crucifixation of Jesus (which by the way wasn't a three point message)! What they did do was to hear about Jesus being raised from the dead and seated in the heavenlies as King on the throne of David. What they did do was cry out, "What must we do to be saved?"

And they then submitted to baptism and joined with the other believers in learning more about their faith through listening to the apostles' teaching. What they did do was realize how much they needed one another and so they continued to have fellowship with each other and break bread in one another's homes. And no one told them to do these things; they just found themselves doing them because they were growing in the life that they now shared in Christ. They were manifesting God's DNA through "the breaking of bread."

Where do we "break bread" together?

Now there is an ambiguity in the expression, "break bread," that is actually fortunate. The question has been raised as to whether this meant that the disciples were "breaking bread" in the since of just eating together in one another's homes; or if it meant that they were celebrating the "Lord's Table" and breaking bread in remembrance of Christ's sacrifice.

The ambiguity actually brings clarity because it was both. For how can you really "break bread" before the Lord in eating from His Table, if you are not willing to "break bread" at the homes of other brethren? If you have fellowship with the Lord and with each other, why wouldn't you want to break bread together in worship at church as well as have such fellowship in one another's homes? If we are serious about being on a journey in Jesus, both settings for "breaking bread" should be seen in our lives together. There was a seamless flow from one to another in the early church. This ought to be our experience today; that is if God's Spirit is at work in us bringing the *Life of Christ*, his *DNA* into our lives.

The Scriptures emphasize this. They want us to see how fellowship with God naturally moves to fellowship with one another in Jesus. And they do this without any apparent tension. "Every day they continued to meet together in the temple courts. They broke bread in their homes and ate together with glad and sincere hearts" (Acts 2:46).

God's DNA brings Christ's Life to Show us we are one in Him!

This intentional usage shows how there was no compartmentalizing of their Christian life from their normal life. They hadn't had time, like believers have today, to separate their "spiritual life" from their "day to day life." They were living on the edge of possibly suffering the same death that Jesus endured. They didn't have time or desire to look at their lives as through their faith meant nothing to their lives. Their faith was their life!

The fact that their lives were on the line showed the reality of how much they believed because no one puts their life on the line for a "compartment" of the rest of one's life. If your life is compartmentalized you just hang out a sign that says, "For Sale" in the area of your life that is causing you grief and hope that someone either takes you up on the offer or they leave you alone. But you can't live like that and the first century believers didn't try to.

Their faith wasn't for sale, because Jesus had moved in and made His home among them and in them and they knew they belonged to him. What a sad commentary on today's secularization of the church that has us thinking it is legitimate for us to have separate areas of life and faith, of church and state, of belonging to Jesus or just being religious. We do that to our spiritual detriment but it was not present in the early church.

God is showing us by their simplicity, the most profound theological truth: To be 'in Jesus,' as individuals, means that we belong to Jesus' Body as well. We are part of the Living Body of Jesus. It is a part of the organic unity that comes from belonging to him. We have *his DNA* and we shouldn't be trying to deny how connected we are. *His Life* is at work within us because we have been given his *Holy Spirit*. God has moved in and we cannot be the same. So if you break bread with one another in church where Jesus is the host, it is perfectly natural to be spending time breaking bread in your homes.

How can we "break bread" when we are "breaking hearts?"

Today people get upset at other believers in their church and yet they all come together on communion Sunday and eat as though nothing was wrong. If they had to first eat dinner together on Saturday night, there might be a better chance to experience the reality of what God intends as we break bread together.

When God and man sat down around that first Table, the evening of our Lord's betrayal, he demonstrated that nothing is as powerful as His love for us. There He was about to be betrayed by one, and denied by all, and yet there Jesus sat to take up the towel and wash his disciples feet. The overwhelming demonstration of that undefeatable love is only matched by His command of us to go and do likewise.

"When he had finished washing their feet, he put on his clothes and returned to his place. 'Do you understand what I have done for you?' He asked them. 'You call me, 'Teacher,' and 'Lord,' and rightly so for that is what I am. Now that I, your Lord and Teacher, have washed your feet, you also should wash one another's feet. I have left you an example that you should do as I have done for you." (John 13:12-15).

This is no mere ironing out of differences. This is a manifestation of the power of God's DNA at work among people who normally couldn't even stand each other. When men who have competed for supremacy over the other disciples as James and John have done; when men have sat in a fishing boat and listened to Peter going on and on about how he has all the faith that is needed to follow Jesus despite the other's lack of faith; when the disciples have followed Jesus with no prospects of their lives ever improving beyond daily bread; Christ' Life is coming to light in their lives.

There is not a natural affection or personal commitment able to survive what they would later face, and yet they did, because the Life of Christ was given them. And they were to remember the example of what happened the night that God and man sat down to break bread and follow Him by showing that kind of love one for another.

We are called to break bread with believers not like us!

Why is it perfectly acceptable for people to spend years in a church and never feel welcomed there? Is it acceptable for people to keep advancing their own agendas and not give a second thought to the advancement of Jesus' Kingdom? Is it acceptable to not accept people because they are different? Do you tell people who want to join your church that they may not 'fit in?' You may think these things don't happen but they do.

How God's heart must continually be broken over attitudes like this. We know this because towards the end of his ministry, when he had already encountered so many divisions within his people; he had to confront the Scribes, the Pharisees, the Sadducees; he even had to confront the attitudes of his own disciples; yet he still cried out over Jerusalem. "O Jerusalem, Jerusalem, you who kill the prophets and stone those sent to you, how often I have longed to gather your children together, as a hen gathers her chicks under her wings, but you were not willing." (Matthew 23:37).

His disciples were going to be the leaders of his church, but they were going to deny him. They would fail him time after time. He knew this, but he still took up a towel and washed their feet. He broke bread with them knowing that it embodied the breaking of his body for us.

Breaking Bread with God and Man

When we break bread with one another, we are entering into *the Life of Christ* at his table. Something mysterious, something spiritual is happening as we sit down with Jesus as our host. But it happens not only between Jesus and us, it happens between us and each other.

We are reminded that God has accepted us. We are reminded that this acceptance comes at the price of his shed blood. But we are also challenged to think about the price we are demanding of others before we accept them. We are reminded that whatever price we are requiring in order to give our fellowship to others, it is an arrogant sacrifice next to Jesus' atoning one.

Look in the mirror and discover who Jesus has loved and invited to his table. What price did he pay for you to sit down with God and man? Whatever price we are asked to pay to sit down at the table of others that we find hard to love is not enough. It never could be enough. But his shed blood has made all of our invitations valid. It has guaranteed the acceptance of all Jesus invites. How dare we encroach upon the rights of others by not welcoming those he has invited?

When there is no difference between the "breaking of bread" in one another's homes and the "breaking of bread" on the Lord's Day together, we will be living before one another as Jesus intended. What we do on the Lord's Day, ought to be a reflection of what is normal for us to do during the week.

We should be breaking break in one another's homes just as we break bread with one another in church gatherings. And this ought to be done for not only our spiritual nourishment, but because we are one Day going to be dining at Heaven's Banquet Table together!

"Blessed are those who are invited to the
wedding supper of the Lamb"
(Revelation 19:9)

Consider how "Breaking Bread" has impacted you

1. I remember when I was very young attending a "foot washing" at a Brethren church in Roanoke, Virginia. I had never been to anything like that! Men and women were separated so there would not be any awkward moments about taking off the shoes and socks of the person next to you and then getting down on your knees to wash their feet as Jesus had done for His disciples. This happened to me 40 years ago and I still remember it! If you haven't experienced this may I suggest you not pass up an opportunity.

2. Another awesome way to experience the Breaking of Bread is to be part of a Jews for Jesus communion

service! Our Jewish brethren bring incredible insight into what the various Old Testament symbols are as represented at the Lords' Table. If you want to know more about this check out their web site or write them and see when they can come your church to hold a service. *www.jewsforjesus.org*

3. Remember that fellowship with each other in the Body of Christ begins with having fellowship with God (1 John 1:3). At the next Lord's Table service ask God to enable your fellowship with Him to be so real, so honest, and so open that you are given new eyes, His eyes, to look upon your brethren in that service and see them as He sees them.

If every believer realized that God wants us to have unhindered fellowship with Him it would make a difference in our desire to have unhindered fellowship with each other. Think about how this might apply to any relationships that you have been struggling with in your church . . . . Read Acts 2:42 again!

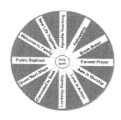

Chapter 10
God's DNA: Earnest Prayer

If there is one critical element of God's DNA that is downplayed in today's ministries it is prayer. Churches have entire ministries developed to make sure that people are "welcomed" and know "how to get started" in their faith. They even have ministries to make sure that new people are assimilated into the ministry so that their gifts are utilized effectively. But ministry after ministry neglects prayer.

When the Holy Spirit was poured out upon the church, one of the *DNA Life characteristics* was the manifestation of *prayer*. We see this from the conception of the church. "They devoted themselves to the apostles' teaching and to fellowship, to the breaking of bread and to prayer" (Acts 2:42).

Prayer was the pattern of life for the early church

We see prayer when the first assaults of persecution came upon the church. Peter and John had been arrested and threatened not to speak any more in the name of Jesus. And after their release, they went back to the brethren and having reported all that had happened to them, "They raised their voices together in prayer to God" (Acts 4:24).

God's affirmation that He had heard and would answer their prayers came as, "The place where they were meeting was shaken. And they were all filled with the Holy Spirit and spoke the word of God boldly" (Acts 4:31).

When the need arose for the early church to appoint deacons, they were set apart by prayer (Acts 6:6).

When Stephen was being stoned to death he found strength to call out to God in prayer. "Lord Jesus receive my spirit." But he also prayed for his executioners. "Lord, do not hold this sin against them" (Acts 7:59-60).

Peter was asked to come at the death of Tabitha. He went to where she lay, "Then got down on his knees and prayed. Turning toward the woman, he said, 'Tabitha, get up.' She opened her eyes and seeing Peter sat up," having been raised from the dead (Acts 9:40).

When Peter was about to be given insight into God's calling the Gentiles to the same faith that the believing Jews had in Jesus as their Messiah; he was found praying on a roof top just before lunch (Acts 10:9). But this was not before Cornelius, a God fearing Gentile, had himself prayed and been told by an angel to send for Peter and listen to the message he would bring to him and his family (Acts 10:2-6).

Paul had been converted during a vision, an imposed prayer time if you will (Acts 9:3)! And as he was praying Ananias was given his own vision to go and find Paul and lay hands on him that his sight might be restored (Acts 9:11).

Later Paul would be set apart along with Barnabas for the mission God had called them to by the church at Antioch fasting and praying for them (Acts 13:3). It became Paul's practice to look for a 'place of prayer' whenever he came upon a new area (Acts 16:13, 16).

And when Paul and Silas were placed in prison for their faith, they could be heard singing hymns and praying to God. This had such an impact upon his jailer at Philippi, especially when God shook the jail by a violent earthquake, that the jailer was converted along with his whole household (Acts 16:25).

And when Paul was completing a phase of his ministry that would set him on a new course of imprisonment and eventual death, he knelt on the beach along with the disciples of Tyre and their wives and children to pray before his departure (Acts 21:3-5). This scene was also repeated with the elders from Ephesus as he knelt along with them to pray for God's mercies and leadership of them all (Acts 20:36).

It is inescapable that *prayer* is part of *the DNA* of the church.

Prayer must again become part of our spiritual lives

If we are to see God do things in our day, we must enter into the joy and warfare of prayer. It is a joy because it takes us into the very presence of God, our Father, who is waiting to hear our hearts and respond to our needs. And it takes us into spiritual battle as we struggle against principalities and powers of the enemy. As Paul exhorts us, "And pray in the Spirit on all occasions with all kinds of prayers and requests. With this in mind, be alert and always keep on praying for all the saints" (Ephesians 6:18).

You cannot look at the early church and not see her as a praying church. Let me ask a simple question, "Does the church today impress you as a praying church?" This is not a wrong question to ask. And I believe the answer is obvious. We are not a praying church.

Perhaps it is because we have become self-justifiers of our actions. We say that prayer is included in our worship services. We say that prayer officially starts all our committee meetings; we open and close with prayer. We make sure that we tell people that we will pray for them when they share things that are burdening them and weighing them down. But just how much are we at prayer for them?

I remember hearing a tape in which Dr. Martyn-Lloyd Jones said that God is moving among His people bringing revival when the phrase, "Oh, God," returns to the vocabulary of prayer in the church.

What he meant was that the church must come to the place of earnest prayer, realizing the desperateness of their circumstances, and pleading with God realizing that unless He moves nothing will happen and if anything happens without His moving it will be of no eternal account.

I long for Dr. Martyn-Lloyd Jones' insight to come true in us. I long for believers in our day to see how desperately they need God to work and unless He works nothing else will do.

But prayer has been replaced by something.

What has the prayer life been replaced with?

I believe it has been replaced by "programs." We don't need God to come. We have organized ourselves on Tuesday and Thursday nights to make sure we implement the latest vision statement. Pastors have become Administrative CEOs who simply carry out the strategy adopted by the leadership and financially supported by the congregation. And if this Pastor isn't able to take us to "the next level," we simply get another one who can.

We have the right church structure, no matter what denomination we happen to be in we all think that ours is the Biblical one. We have the right theology, for the same reason. We have sent all our "key people" to the proper seminars. And now all we need do is properly communicate to the people our vision for ministry and things will take off. Where we are going and why it will be better no one seems to know, but we will take off anyway!

But *the DNA of prayer* declares that unless God builds the house, its laborers labor in vain (Psalm 127:1)! We take seriously that our life comes only from Christ and unless we abide in him through prayer we will bear no fruit; none at all.

Jesus said, "I am the vine; you are the branches. If a man remains in me and I in him, he will bear much fruit; apart from me you can do nothing" (John 15:5). We believe this because we believe Jesus, so we pray.

When did you last cry out to God?

In the Old Testament we find all kinds of prayers. David's prayers were often more of a crying out to God than anything else. Today people seem to be concerned about the form of our prayer more than they are about praying. If we fear getting it wrong we will simply not pray. But God isn't interested in our form of prayer. He simply wants us to pray. He wants to hear our hearts.

David was not afraid to express himself by crying out to God with whatever was on his heart. You can read the Psalms and find over 50 times when it is said he cried out to God. Here are a few examples of David crying out to God, "Listen to my cry for help, my King and my God, for to you I pray" (Psalm 5:2). "For he who avenges blood remembers; he does not ignore the cry of the afflicted" (Psalm 9:12). "Hear, O LORD, my righteous plea; listen to my cry. Give ear to my prayer—it does not rise from deceitful lips" (Psalm 17:1). "O my God, I cry out by day, but you do not answer, by night, and am not silent" (Psalm 22:2). "For he has not despised or disdained the suffering of the afflicted one; he has not hidden his face from him but has listened to his cry for help" (Psalm 22:24).

You can't read these and not realize that David's prayers expressed a heart for God. But neither can you read them and not realize that David was honest about what he was feeling so he "cried" out to God in prayer. This made David's prayers honest. He wasn't afraid to let God know what was on his heart. It would shock us if we hear his honestly in most churches. It should not but it would.

In the New Testament, Jesus gave us an example of how we should pray when he said, "This, then, is how you should pray: "'Our Father in heaven, hallowed be your name, your kingdom come, your will be done on earth as it is in heaven. Give us today our daily bread. Forgive us our debts, as we also have forgiven our debtors. And lead us not into temptation, but deliver us from the evil one" (Matthew 6:9-13). By this example Jesus told us our prayers should be simple and unpretentious.

The apostle Paul tells us something else. He tells us that when we pray we don't always know how to pray, but that's ok. Paul tells us, "Not only so, but we ourselves, who have the firstfruits of the Spirit, groan inwardly as we wait eagerly for our adoption as sons, the redemption of our bodies . . . In the same way, the Spirit helps us in our weakness. We do not know what we ought to pray for, but the Spirit himself intercedes for us with groans that words cannot express. And he who searches our hearts knows the mind of the Spirit, because the Spirit intercedes for the saints in accordance with God's will" (Romans 8:23, 26-27).

Like David, we cry out to God but Paul says that our groans and longings get translated by the Holy Spirit so that our prayers are accomplishing the will of God. What an awesome thing for us to know that the Holy Spirit is himself interceding for us, taking all of our weaknesses into account, and making our prayers heard before the throne of God in accordance to his will! So we call out asking for God to do in us and for us what we can never do for ourselves: advance the Kingdom of God. And we so pray energetically and without hesitation because God will hear us and he will answer our prayers!

Consider how "Prayer" impacts your life

1. You may not think that you pray very much, and maybe you don't, but there was a time in your life when you were learning to pray. Do you remember when that was? It was when your life was falling apart and you

knew that you needed God so you cried out to Him for mercy . . . and He showed it to you.

Or it may have been when you were facing that health crisis and you felt that you were going to die so you asked God to grant you grace . . . and He has. Or it was when that friend of yours lost his job and you felt that if God didn't do something in his life now he would never be open to listen again . . . so you prayed for him and you continue to long for God's work in his life. You see you pray more than you realize it, you really do!

What you need to see is just how much God's *Life* is in you; his *Spirit's DNA* mark in your life has caused you by nature, by your new spiritual nature, to want to cry out to God! Even if you don't know what to pray for . . . even if you get it wrong in praying . . . you don't have to worry because the Spirit knows our hearts' groans and He knows God's will and He takes the two and works them out together . . . our hearts' groans being brought to right expression before God so that God's will is in turn accomplished in us!

So what are you waiting for . . . get to praying!

2. What can you do today to pray for your spouse and some deep need that they have, that they struggle with, that they may have even given up on . . . lift them before our Father and see what God will do for them too!

3. What is happening in the ministry that you attend? Is there a prayer ministry? Get involved with it this week! If there isn't a prayer ministry, here's how you can start one . . .

Call the Pastor and let him know that you are going to be praying for him every morning at 5 a.m. and that you would like to know what he would like you to pray for him about! After he recovers from passing out on the floor, he will pick up the phone receiver and thank you!

Believe me in saying as a pastor how I valued it every time someone told me they were praying for me. Why not be the one who starts a prayer ministry in your church? Start praying for your pastor!

4. Subscribe to The Voice of Martyrs by email and they will send you a regular list of persecuted Christians you can pray for every day! *www.persecution.com* You can't read about Christians who are going through so much and remaining faithful to Jesus without realizing the God's DNA creates living cells in the Body of Christ that are always active, always multiplying, and always remaining true to their spiritual DNA. It challenges all of us who think that we have tough times to pray for those who really do!

Chapter 11
God's DNA: Awe in Worship

The first message I ever preached at seminary was about the importance of true worship. I was taking my first course from Dr. Edmund Clowney on preaching. Seminaries are supposed to "prepare you for ministry." Preaching was certainly going to be a key component in that. I was grateful that I had the privilege to be under the direction of Dr. Clowney, the President of Westminster Seminary.

The problem was I was scared to death. The text I chose was Matthew 15:8-9. It was especially close to home for me because I was an assistant pastor and I had already come up against "the traditions of men" that were being imposed on people. The leadership had made a "covenant" and required all church leaders to sign it. It didn't matter whether you were in the choir or taught Sunday school, or whether you were an officer or volunteer worker; if you were involved in ministry in any way you had to sign their covenant or not be able to stay in that ministry.

This was my first position and I wanted to be submissive to the leaders in the church. I also depended upon this ministry for an income to help our family needs. So not knowing what else to do I signed it along with everyone else. My wife was also forced to sign it as well because she helped me in my ministry. But just how far do you have to go to fit within traditions of various churches?

At some point you are going to have to deal with the question, "What does the Bible teach about this?" And if the answer to that puts you in conflict with a particular "tradition" that binds your conscious in a way that the Word of God does not bind it, you are going to have to make a decision about "worship." The reason you are going to have to make a decision about "worship" is because you are going to have to decide if you value the "traditions of men" more than you value "worshipping God" and being free to follow him.

When rules become more important than worship

I know believers who are Republican and others who are Democrat. I know believers who are conservative and others who are liberal. I have heard Steve Brown of Key Life Ministry say he is politically to the right of Genghis Kong! Tony Campolo is known for many of his more liberal views of politics.[6] But Steve and Tony respect each other and they are not involved in character assignation just because they may want to show each other up in a political debate!

There's something else I have learned. I've learned that there is a very real temptation to get more passionate about our "view" of something, our "teachings" on something, and our "rules" about something, than to get fired up about what God has spoken!

How sad it is that we go to war over "teachings" and "rules" of men when the ministry of Jesus was to end all hostility. He came to set prisoners free. He came to take us to God, not to condemn us for not getting to Him before. He came to provide, by His own death upon the cross, a means of forgiveness for our violating the only rules that really mattered: God's law.

---

6   Tony Campolo, Wikipedia The Free Encyclopedia, article on Tony Campolo tagged since October 2006

In Jesus we have God's wrath appeased and turned away. In Him there is no condemnation. In Him we have the only mediator between God and men. And He is our brother and not ashamed to call us family.

Yet in the church there seems to be this propensity to re-establish rules. Rules that tell believers what is and is not acceptable. There are rules that tell us why we never will fit in with others who love the rules. There are rules that separate one church from another church, one denomination from another denomination, and consequently one believer from another believer.

Are we in love with our traditions or Jesus?

When you go through some of these things, it makes you want to step back and say, "Are we more passionate about our "rules" than we are for Jesus?" I hope that's not the case, but I fear sometimes it is.

You know that's the case if you decide that their "rules" aren't for you because as soon as you try and speak to someone in a position of power, you are quickly told that your views will get you a one way ticket out of that ministry! It doesn't matter how effective your ministry may have been or how long you may have been doing it. To break one of their rules constitutes immediate anathema!

How is it that we have come to believe that worship isn't enough? How is it that we think we can help God out by making up our own rules so that people will be right to worship? How is it that all of your sins can be cleansed by the blood of Jesus and yet you still stand condemned because you are told you don't measure up to a committee decision?

You can be served up as dead meat before a church because of some rule the leadership has passed and yet no one seems to notice that we all stand condemned by the only rules that matter: God's Law!

Are we showing more reverence for our orders than for God's ordinances? You know that we are when our passions are stirred more by them than by Jesus. No wonder we have a hard time worshipping because we are all so worried about something else to warrant another rebuke. Are we now going to be judged by even inadvertent violations of men's rules when the King of heaven has dismissed all charges?

I am glad God answers that for us. Paul writes, "Therefore, there is now no condemnation for those who are in Christ Jesus, because through Christ Jesus the law of the Spirit of life set me free from the law of sin and death" (Romans 8:1-2). "Who will bring a charge against those whom God has chosen? It is God who justifies. Who is he that condemns? Christ Jesus who died-more than that, who was raised to life-is at the right hand of God and is also interceding for us" (Romans 8:33-34).

What's more important?

If you break God's law, He offers forgiveness! "If we confess our sins, He is faithful and just and will forgive us our sins" (1 John 1:9). But if we break the rules of men in the church, they are held over us, kept on file, and brought out at any moment chosen to prove that we have a record of not playing well with others!

Yet who can claim that their "teachings" or "rules" are promoting things that are truly spiritual? Paul says, "Since you died with Christ to the basic principles of this world, why as though you still belonged to it, do you submit to its rules: 'Do not handle! Do not taste! Do not touch!' These are all destined to perish with use, because they are based on human commands and teachings. Such regulations indeed have an appearance of wisdom, with their self-imposed worship, their false humility and their harsh treatment of the body, but they lack any value in restraining sensual indulgence." (Colossians 2:20-23)

No standard we can come up with can promote spirituality. That's what Paul says. And why is that? Because no law, not even God's law had the power to change anyone's life. It only had the power to point out sin and condemn a man because of it. As the author of Hebrews said, "The law made nothing perfect" (Hebrews 7:19).

So why is all this fuss made? Because men make rules to tell us how to "really" get it right. They tell us what is required for us to do in order to gain acceptance. But the gospel proclaims that God has accepted us in Christ because He kept God's law and died to pay the penalty of us who daily break it! And when you understand what Jesus has done for you, rules of men only put up barriers to keep us separated from God; to rate our performance; to evaluate our spirituality; and because of this they inevitably keep us from simply "worshipping God!"

Pentecost shattered all the shackles that had held men captive!

At Pentecost Peter pointed out that all of his hearers were culpable for the death of Christ. But he also pointed out that God used their wicked acts to accomplish the saving of His people. "This man was handed over to you by God's set purpose and foreknowledge; and you, with the help of wicked men, put him to death by nailing him to the cross. But God raised him from the dead, freeing him from the agony of death, because it was impossible for death to keep its hold on him" (Acts 2:23-24).

And having heard that the One they crucified had now been exalted by God to His right hand where he was seated on the throne of David in heaven, they realized that they had condemned the One who is the Lord of Glory and they cried out for mercy. The fruit of their repentance issued into their worship of God for He had been so gracious to them. "Everyone was filled with awe . . . Ever day they continued to meet together in the temple courts . . . praising God and enjoying favor of all the people" (Acts 2:43, 46-47).

Worship was part of their *DNA*. They demonstrated it through their spontaneous desire to worship the God who had saved them from all of their sins that even their religious rules and traditions had no power to do. *God's Dynamic New Activity (DNA)* was obvious as *the Holy Spirit* continued to bring *the Life of Christ* to God's people.

Their worship cut through all the traditions that have been such a part of their lives. Sometimes we layer our traditions so thick over our view of how we should worship that we become preoccupied with "getting worship right" rather than just worshipping! God isn't impressed by "rules taught by men." He wants our hearts . . . open and full of worship towards him!

How sad that many churches are preoccupied with power struggles, personality differences, and programs. When we are missing God's best by simply not worshipping! What is keeping us from such joy, from such simple pleasure, of just enjoying God and worshipping him for who he is! Why are we preoccupied with someone else's agendas or preferences? Make the choice to worship God and experience *God's DNA* for the church!

God is teaching me that none of the preoccupations of men matter. The only thing that matters is coming to know him who alone matters. And his name is Jesus.

Oh come, let us worship him!

Over the past seven months my wife and I have had the opportunity to visit congregations of a variety of denominational backgrounds. It has been a wonderful experience for many reasons, but what has been the most beautiful is in experiencing "worship" from the perspective of these brethren.

Some were Baptist, some Independent, some were Methodist, some were Pentecostal and some were Presbyterian, but all were expressing God's DNA of worship. The reason is because God's Spirit is still calling men to a Life relationship with Jesus! And when that happens, men and women, boys and girls, and little ones, find themselves worshipping him!

It wasn't a particular style of worship that made us know that Jesus was present. Some were very formal and used only hymns written from times past. Others were quite contemporary and never used a hymn at all. They used video and power-point presentations with large screens and TV monitors throughout the sanctuary.

Some services used only the organ. Some had a full band with drums and keyboard. Some services used contemporary music. Some were blended combining the contemporary songs with traditional hymns to compliment the sermon. Most all of the ministries had a worship team leading the services.

But what we experienced, regardless of the particular denominational preference, was a shared ministry of the Holy Spirit in bringing the Life of Jesus to His people. The Spirit is creating worship upon the lips of God's children who cannot help but praise him. And this worship transcends denominations, traditions, and styles of ministry because it is part of God's DNA in the lives of his kids.

Praise at Pentecost

If we would take a fresh look at what was happening at Pentecost when the first fruits of Christ's work was being harvested through the Spirit baptizing believers with God's presence in their lives; if we would realize that fundamental to his work in us is unabated and unhindered worship; we would again experience the Life of Jesus among us.

We wouldn't get hung up about whether we thought others were getting it right. We would realize that none of us ever did but that is why Jesus came. Jesus showed us how to worship by freeing our hearts to praise the God who saved us. Once, we were formerly held captive by Satan due to our sin, and Jesus has now set us free from all condemnation that we might live in the joy of being God's kids!

Brethren at Pentecost were experiencing worship. Awe was being created in their souls for all that God was doing among them. They were learning to worship in Spirit and truth (John 4:24). The Spirit was opening their eyes to what God was doing in Jesus; and the apostles teaching was helping them grow in their understanding of God's grace (Acts 2:16-16, 42). Praise could be heard in the temple courts and in the streets of Jerusalem as they traveled back and forth to their homes (Acts 2:43, 46). May God be gracious and fill our city streets with such praise!

Consider how "Worship" should be impacting your life:

1. It is so very important for us to worship the God who has created us and redeemed us! Worship is the preoccupation of heaven and it ought to be the preoccupation of our hearts here on earth. Read Revelation 4 through Revelation 5 and see this for yourself.

2. Jesus said, "Yet a time is coming and has now come when the true worshippers will worship the Father in spirit and truth, for they are the kind of worshippers the Father seeks. God is spirit and his worshippers must worship in spirit and in truth" (John 4:23-24).

   Among other things this means that there must be no pretense or hypocrisy in our worship. We must have no agenda. He is God and we reverence Him for who He is and what He has done and what He is going to do. Ask God to make this more and more real as you gather with other believers this week to worship (Hebrews 10:25).

3. Another reason we stand in awe of God is the way He brings us to understand that we can adore Him for bringing us to the place in our journey that we trust Him implicitedly for even the hard times that may come to us. Our communities need to see a people of hope in days of despair. They need to see a people celebrating grace when they do make the effort to visit a service. They need to see that even if we are facing struggles we are still finding our joy in Jesus. They need to see *God's DNA of worship* active in us!"

As believers we have to again become preoccupied with Jesus! We have to ask the Holy Spirit to fill our lives and enable us to worship the Father in spirit and in truth. God called us to share *the Life in Jesus* with people and there is no better way to share that then for them to experience worship in a body of believers whose lives are focused on Christ (1st Corinthians 14:25).

Consider what things may be in your own life that you may have a personal preference for but which really aren't something that God has forbidden. Are you keeping a friend or family member from hearing about Jesus because all they hear from you is a list of "your rules?"

Ask God to work his *DNA* grace of *worship* in you so that *Jesus becomes your preoccupation in all that you do* including your sharing him with others. If you can't live freely before him in your own conscience, how are others going to hear a message of freedom from you? Read Romans 14:17-18. Ask God for perspective and balance in your life and ministry. Don't let anything hinder the call for all of us to, "Worship!"

4. A great ministry that will bring balance to your worship: See Steve Brown's ministry at *www.keylife.org* or visit one of his speaking engagements near you!

5. You might ask Charlie and Ruth Jones to your church and share their ministry in drama. If that doesn't make you laugh and have fun in worshipping God again, you may need therapy! *www.peculiarpeople.com*

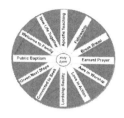

Chapter 12
God's DNA: Love in Action

I don't know any Christian who would not want to do the right thing. We all sin. As the Apostle Paul said, "We all sin and fall short of the glory of God" (Romans 3:23). But believers also affirm that their lives have been changed by Jesus. We are not perfect but we are forgiven. And that forgiveness we've received from God has made us better people. We don't want to sin because our propensity and desire to sin has been replaced by a propensity and desire to please God.

But having said that, every believer wants it to be clearly understood that any goodness seen in us; any act of kindness that we have shown; any change seen in us; has come directly from God as a result of his grace to us. And believers want it to be further understood that we aren't seeking to be good in order to gain a place in heaven because heaven has already been given us as a result of the merit of Jesus Christ that we have received by faith in him.

These two things, the fact that we have been changed but that change hasn't come as a result of anything we have achieved by ourselves; and the fact that this change in us has resulted in our lives actually being enabled to do good things, though even those good things are being done as a result of God's work in us; have been articulated by Paul when he writes, "For it is by grace have you been saved-through faith, and this not from yourselves, it is a gift of God-not by works, so that no one can boast. For we are God's workmanship, created in Christ Jesus to do good works, which God has prepared in advance for us to do" (Ephesians 2:8-10).

Grace changes us, it really does!

This may appear to be a bit of a balancing act; but God's act of grace in us is one that brings us to act in grace. We are brought into his family by an adoption process that he initiates. "He predestined us to be adopted as his sons through Jesus Christ, in accordance with his pleasure and will" (Ephesians 1:5).

We are given spiritual armor that can protect us in spiritual battles so that we can accomplish all that God has for us to do as believers. "Put on the full armor of God so that you can take your stand against the devil's schemes" (Ephesians 6:11).

And we will be watched over as his Spirit continues to translate our deepest needs into being achieved in accordance with God's greatest design on us. "In the same way, the Spirit helps us in our weakness. We do not know what we ought to pray for, but the Spirit himself intercedes for us with groans that words cannot express. And he who searches our hearts knows the mind of the Spirit, because the Spirit intercedes for the saints in accordance with God's will" (Romans 8:26-27).

This means that *God's grace design* is in every part of our lives. It includes our coming to faith in Christ, being equipped to live for Christ, and being protected in the spiritual battles we fight for Christ (Ephesians 1:6; 4:7; 6:10).

In all that we are and in all that God calls us to do, he is fashioning us to know his grace, to live out of grace, and to be gracious with others. "For we are God's workmanship, created in Christ Jesus to do good works, which God prepared in advance for us to do" (Ephesians 2:10).

God is fashioning us by his *Spirit* so that we might experience his grace, but he is also fashioning us so that we might be gracious to others. As his grace is at work in us, and as we share that grace with others, they will begin to see for themselves what grace is. This is why it is so important for us to demonstrate *God's love in action*. It is part of *the Holy Spirit's DNA* in ministry.

Grace brings God's love to us so that we can bring God's love to others

When you come to know the love of God you want to share the love of God with others. This is more than just a gospel presentation. It cannot be just talk. The apostle John affirmed this when he said, "Dear children, let us not love with words or tongue but with actions and in truth" (1 John 3:18).

John was the disciple known as, "The disciple whom Jesus loved" (John 13:23). He had more insights into what Jesus meant about love than any of the other disciples did. And John said that it wasn't about preaching to people, but loving people with actions of love that show God's unconditional love for sinners.

We have forgotten the simplicity of this *DNA* present in Jesus' ministry and have made ministry just about what we believe. But if what we believe isn't impacting our lives; if what we believe isn't being used of God to impact the lives of others so that they come to see the love of God through us; then there is a fundamental question as to whether we even understand the faith we profess to have ourselves! John says, "If anyone has material possessions and sees his brother in need but has no pity on him, how can the love of God be in him?" (1 John 3:17) Gospel truth must issue forth into gospel action.

Love is Action reveals whether Love is known!

Did you know that of all the things Jesus will ask of us when we face him in the final judgment, none of them have to do with what we can articulate about our faith? There is no theological test, no history of the church exam, no philosophy of ministry defended. When Jesus has men come before him on the last day, the Bible says that he will ask them whether they have cared for other believers or not. The Bible says that God will be in asking us whether we took the time, the energy and the resources at our disposal to demonstrate his *love in action* to our brethren when we saw them in need (Matthew 25:31-46).

I know of churches where people have said that they don't want too many "needy people" in their church because it keeps them from accomplishing what they feel their mission is!

Hey, here's a news flash! God loves needy people! And our mission is to minister to them! If we aren't ministering to the needy there is a real question about whether we know the love of God ourselves.

John has already warned that the failure of showing the love of God actually reveals a lack of the love of God in our own lives when he said, "If anyone has material possessions and sees his brother in need but has no pity on him, how can the love of God be in him?" (1 John 4:17) But in the last picture Jesus gives us of the final judgment, he warns us that failure to demonstrate the love of God in practical ways is the basis of being eternally condemned because it reveals that anyone who lives like this could not possibly know God.

Those who have shown love in practical ways demonstrate that they have really come to know the love of God. "Then the King will say to those on his right, 'Come, you who are blessed by my Father; take your inheritance, the kingdom prepared for you since the creation of the world. For I was hungry and you gave me something to eat, I was thirsty and you gave me something to drink, I was a stranger and you invited me in, I needed clothes and you clothed me, I was sick and you looked after me, I was in prison and you came to visit me.' Then the righteous will answer him, 'Lord, when did we see you hungry and feed you, or thirsty and give you something to drink? When did we see you a stranger and invite you in; or needing clothes and clothe you? When did we see you sick or in prison and go to visit you?' The King will reply, 'I tell you the truth, whatever you did for one of the least of these brothers of mine, you did for me." (Matthew 25:34-40)

But those who fail to care for the brethren's practical needs show that they don't love God by not demonstrating love for people in practical ways. "Then he will say to those on his left, 'Depart from me, you who are cursed, into the eternal fire prepared for the devil and his angels. For I was hungry and you gave me nothing to eat, I was thirsty and you gave me nothing to drink, I was a stranger and you did not invite me in, I needed clothes and you did not clothe me, I was sick and in prison and you did not look after me.' They also will answer, 'Lord, when did we see you hungry or thirsty or a stranger or needing clothes or sick or in prison, and did not help you?' "He will reply, 'I tell you the truth, whatever you did not do for one of the least of these, you did not do for me.' Then they will go away to eternal punishment, but the righteous to eternal life." (Matt. 25:42-46)

These are some of the most incredible passages in all of Scripture that show us just how important it is to demonstrate *God's love in action*. When you compare these verses with what we see happening in Acts, as Jesus pours out the *Holy Spirit* upon His church, we see the church living out of the *Life of Christ*. We see the *DNA*, the *Dynamic New Activity of God's Spirit* in *the life of God's people*.

The apostle James confirms this in his no nonsense letter when he adds his voice to say, "What good is it, my brothers, if a man claims to have faith but has no deeds? Can such faith save him? Suppose a brother or sister is without clothes and daily food. If one of you says to him, 'Go, I wish you well; keep warm and well fed,' but does nothing about his physical needs, what good is it? In the same way, faith by itself, if it is not accompanied by action is dead" (James 2:14-17).

You can't just 'talk' about a person's needs and do nothing and call yourself a believer! Your action is speaking heaps about what you actually 'believe!' To put it another way, when you look at the lives of those who truly know God, you are going to see their lives working out God's call upon them by ministering to the needs of others in very practical ways.

Abraham's faith was tested in practical ways

Even Abraham, when God tested him to see if he really did fear God above all things, did not go through a theological exam, but he went through an experiential exam, an exam in life. James says that when you look at Abraham's life, you see his faith in action. You see no incongruity between what he says he believed and how he lived. James makes the point that Abraham's life is proof that you have to be living what you believe for your beliefs to demonstrate *Life*. "You foolish man, do you want evidence that faith without works is useless? Was not our ancestor Abraham considered righteous for what he did when he offered his son Isaac on the altar? You see that his faith and his actions were working together and his faith was made complete by what he did." (James 2:20-22)

This is critical to understand why *Love in Action* is part of God's DNA. It is not a superficial part or an incidental part of God's genetic code. It is what the *Life of Christ* looks like as it is manifested in believers. It is central and as critical as what a person's theology is; or what their fellowship is like with God and other believers; or what their prayer life really says about them.

The litmus test for how a person is making their journey in Jesus can be seen in how they minister to others in meeting their needs. These words seem out of place in today's church culture where demands are made that, "The church must meet my needs or I will find one that does!"

The words of Jesus are the opposite! If you are not concerned to the point of actually getting involved in meeting the needs of others, you don't understand what knowing God means! God has not put himself at your disposal to meet your needs. He has put you at his disposal to meet the needs of others. The church in Acts manifested this *DNA* and we are told by Luke that, "there was not a needy person among them," because they cared for each other (Acts 4:34). They demonstrated *God's love in action!*

God's love in action may not be noticed by others but it is noticed by God!

It doesn't have to be an effort that others would recognize as note-worthy. Jesus said it can be as small as a cup of cold water given in His name (Matthew 10:42). But it does have to be an effort that makes a real difference to someone in need; to someone who would begin to wonder if God loved them had this gift not been given. It might be a meal, "you gave me something to eat," it might be some water, "you gave me something to drink," it might be an invitation to come in your home and stretch out on your lounge, "you invited me in." But it will be something to show that you wanted others to know the care and love of God.

In today's church world in which we need to make sure that people really do believe the Bible, that they really do believe the fundamentals of the importance of a relationship with Christ and seeing the Bible as God's map for our journey; it is critical that we not forget *God's DNA* is also seen in our showing God's *"Love in Action."*

Love is visible, practical, and personal. It may be as simple as that cup of cold water or it may be as costly as the selling of our property so that others not suffer from the hardships on their journeys. But it will touch people's lives in ways that a sermon never could. This is seen in the early church at Pentecost as Jesus poured out *His Life-giving Spirit, His DNA,* upon the church and people demonstrated his *love in action.* "Selling their possessions and goods, they gave to anyone as he had need" (Acts 2:45).

Can you imagine how the church would impact the communities in which she has erected her buildings, if every believer in that ministry was watched over, cared for, and supported by the Body of Christ when they fell upon hard times? Buildings are great to provide the means to facilitate ministry, but financing them isn't to stop the ministry of mercy that God has called us to have.

Hypocrisy or Help?

The biggest criticism leveled against the church has always been, "The church is full of hypocrites." What if our lives left no doubt about the love of God because what we said we had in our hearts was seen in our lives as we served one another. I think that this is what Jesus meant when he said, "A new command I give you: Love one another. As I have loved you, so you must love one another. By this all men will know that you are my disciples, if you love one another" (John 13:34-35).

The greatest evangelization of our communities comes from the visible realization of love among us! We have talked long and hard about the love of God in this country, but I ask you, "Have people seen the love of God in us by how we treat one another?"

If the church got as serious about actually caring for one another the way she is serious about building buildings this nation would be changed! It might bring the biggest revival this nation has ever seen. Imagine no one being able to bring a charge of hypocrisy against us because our love for one another would be too obvious to condemn. Peter tells us to keep a clear conscious by how we respond to criticism so that, "those who speak maliciously against your good behavior in Christ may be ashamed of their slander" (1 Pet. 3:16).

We are undermining our own witness when we don't love one another

The problem hasn't been that churches have such terrible theology that they don't even know who Jesus is. There are churches like that, but that is not representative of the majority of congregations that seek to be grounded in the historic Christian faith. The problem isn't so much what we believe as it is the disconnection that is so often present between our faith and how we live.

The apostle John said, "It has given me great joy to find some of your children walking in the truth, just as the Father commanded us" (2nd John 4). Knowing the truth of God is critical for us to be able to walk in it. "Your word is a lamp to my feet and a light to my path" (Psalm 119:105). But the intent of God is that we not only know the truth but actually walk in it. "But if anyone obeys his word, God's love is truly made complete in him. This is how we know we are in him: Whoever claims to live in him must walk as Jesus did" (1st John 2:5-6).

It is part of God's Dynamic Nucleus Activity that his Spirit manifests God's love in action in the Life of the church. When we show God's love in action we embody the way Jesus walked and in so doing we reflect his image.

John reminded the early disciples, "I ask that we love one another. And this is love: that we walk in obedience to his commands. As you heard from the beginning, his command is that you walk in love" (2nd John 5-6). And what is walking in love? Ministering in practical needs to the needs of your brethren is walking in love. "Dear children, let us not love with words or tongue but with actions and in truth" (1st John 3:18).

Truth sets the Direction but Love sets the Pace

When you consider your own journey in Jesus, remember, truth sets the direction for your journey, but love must set the pace! John calls us to "walk in the truth" but do so in a way that demonstrates that this "walk is in love." "And this is love: that we walk in obedience to His commands. As you have heard from the beginning, his command is that you walk in love" (2nd John 6).

If you are pursuing "truth" in a "way" that runs over people, that makes demands upon them, that forces unloving consequences; if you so teach people in such a way that their hearts are bound in the bondage of what they keep failing to do, rather than showing them the love of God that can empower them to start again; then you are not ministering in the way of Jesus.

What does a Walk of Love look like?

The Bible says a lot about what a walk in love looks like: "Love keeps no records of wrongs" (1st Corinthians 13:5). "Accept one another, then just as Christ accepted you" (Romans 15:7). "Carry each other's burdens, and in this way you will fulfill the law of Christ" (Galatians 6:2). "A new command I give you: Love one another. As I have loved you, so you must love one another. By this all men will know that you are my disciples, if you love one another" (John 13:34).

"This is how we know what love is: Jesus Christ laid down his life for us. And we ought to lay down our lives for our brothers. If anyone has material possessions and sees his brother in need but has no pity on him, how can the love of God be in him? Dear children, let us not love with words or tongue but with actions and in truth!" (1st John 3:16-18) *Is God's DNA of "love in action" being seen in you? Can it be seen in the ministry that you have?*

Consider how "Love in Action" has impacted your life:

1. Churches that are alive with God's DNA demonstrate Love in Action. They don't just "preach" it, they live it. In one way or another, their practical motto is, "Just Do It!" Your city might have a "Mission" you can get involved with that helps feed and clothe people. Or there might be a Habitat of Humanity ministry near you that can help house families. But seek opportunities to help:

a. See *www.habitat.org* for a community ministry you can get involved.

b. Or check out *www.redeemer.com* for a ministry that has made an impact upon the people that are hurting in the city of New York with its ministry of Mercy and Justice.

2. But isn't there something you can do in your own family as well? How about doing those dishes for your wife! Or, ladies, how about taking out the trash! And for all of you kids out there, give dad the shock of his life by offering to help him mow the grass!

There are always things that we can do to show the love of God in action. You won't have to look very far . . . why God might just bring someone across your path today . . . Read Luke 10:25-37 and, "Go and do likewise!"

Epilogue

The Journey in Jesus has Begun!

www.journeyinjesus.com

God never intended that we journey alone. When God could no longer walk with Adam in the cool of the Garden because of Adam's sin, God was not deterred in His determination for man to come to be restored to fellowship with him. At the cost of His own Son's blood, God determined that the love He had posessed from all eternity for His people be secured. And now because Jesus came and walked among us, we have been given the privilege of grace and the power to walk with God once again. This is not achieved it is given. It is all of grace. But it is a grace that has come. God took initiative for us to be redeemed and God has taken initiative for us to remain in fellowship with him on our journeys.

He has done this by the pouring out his Holy Spirit into our lives. When the Holy Spirit came at Pentecost, Christ literally poured out *his Life*, his *Life-Giving Spirit*, upon His church. His Presence in us shows itself through *Dynamic Neculus Activity*, the powerful-core-ministry of the *Holy Spirit*. *Life* has literally come to us, *Christ's Life* and we are changed forever marked by the *Holy Spirit* as being one of God's kids. His *DNA* is undeniable. He cannot and would not deny his own. God lives in us. And God is fashioning us right now for His purpose. He is using us and he will fulfull his purpose for us!

The various stands of *DNA (Dynamic Neucleus Acitivity)* of the *Holy Spirit* that I have covered in this book are by no means comprehensive. The entire genetic code has not been mapped! But we have made a start at looking, in a way perhaps that you haven't thought about before, at the Body as being more, so much more, than the programs she runs.

The Body of Christ is filled with *the Life of God* and while we may observe characteristics that reflect *the Holy Spirit's activity* at a genetic level, we may never reduce *Life* to our observations. But it is important to see what God is doing. To that end I have offered these various strands as *DNA*. But these cannot be simply reproduced like a model plane. God's *Spirit does this work* as he brings the very *Life of Christ* to dwell in us and to change us at our spiritual genetic level.

It is important that this not be just another model even though for practical reasons I have called it the *"Spirit Life Paradigm."* We must look beyond the visible world of church programs and personalities to a world that has more *Life* than we can imagine. A *Life* that is comprised of many workings of the *Holy Spirit that it will leave us in awe of God.* This is a *"Spirit Life Paradigm"* whose genetic strands are just some of the *Holy Spirit's DNA* in us. But they are at work in us as sons and daughters in Christ even when we are unaware of it (See diagram).

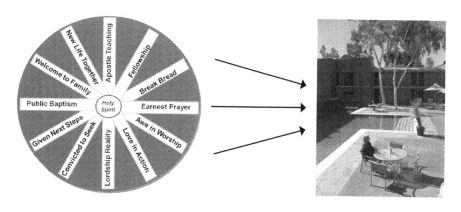

God's DNA   *Individual Believers*

Taken individualy in a person's life, these strands of *DNA* are powerful and transforming because they reflect Christ's life in us. Taken coorporately as they genetically build God's work within *the Body of Christ* they reflect Ezekiel's dry bones coming to *Life!* The *Life* they express is undeniable. But it is also predictable. Not in the sense of "sameness" that becomes another lifeless tradition; but in the sense of being "consistent" because no matter what the Body is dressed with denominationally, it remains *God's Body* with *God's Life*, the *Spirit's DNA* breathed into her.

We see this working out in the life of God's church as the Holy Spirit multiplies the life of Christ. This is a work of God. It bears his Spirit's signature.

This doesn't mean that we only observe what God is doing (John 5:17). Christians are part of *God's living organism* called *the Body of Christ.* We are part of what God is doing (1ˢᵗ Corinthians 12:27). And because we are part of his body the *Spirit's DNA* is at work in us as he indwells his church (Ephesians 2:21-22).

The Spirit writes God's law upon our hearts and begins to transform us into the image of Jesus. But we are also part of what the Spirit is doing in the whole of the Body as this same process is at work. We have God's Spirit manifesting his DNA in us, but this is in the context of the Spirit's work within the whole of the body of Christ. As Paul puts it, "From him the whole body, joined and held together by every supporting ligament, grows and builds itself up in love, as each part does its work (Ephesians 4:16)."

This is important to note because God's life within us is working in a way that the life of the body of Christ is also benefited. You might say as individuals we are one cell within a cluster of cells, which is the local church; within the context of a body, as represented by the Spirit's work in a city or community; and that is within the context of what God is doing in the world.

The Spirit's work, his DNA, is always the same. He will be working to bring about the same manifestations of his life no matter where he is at work. His work becomes obvious regardless of the particular denomination or ministry or nation because he brings *Christ's life* to us.

Three Spirit Life Steps you can take

There are three *Spirit Life-steps* that any individual or congregation can take on a journey in Jesus. The first is to *proclaim* his Lordship remembering not only his life, death and resurrection, but also his ascension, enthronement, and outpouring of his Spirit. The second step we can take is to *pray* for the Holy Spirit to work in us. We do this boldly knowing God has promised to come into our lives and enable us to not only be transformed into Christ's image but to also be empowered to fulfill Christ's purpose for us. And thirdly, we simply *put into practice* the things God's Spirit is leading us to do. These will always be in line with God's revealed will in the Bible. But they will also be creative in seeing God's truth applied in unique ways to our particular journeys.

God has guaranteed that he will complete his work here on earth through the lives of his people as they are empowered by his Spirit. We have the privilege to see that work as we understand how *the Life of Christ* has been poured out upon his church through His Spirit. This is manifested as God sovereignly moves in his church to bring about Christ's kingdom here on earth. This happens wherever God's Spirit is free to move in different congregations.

So why wouldn't we want to see God do more things in our midst? Don't you long to see God's name honored in our churches and in our communities? Consider the following diagramn and join me in praying for God to do in our midst what we all know will never happen unless he works!

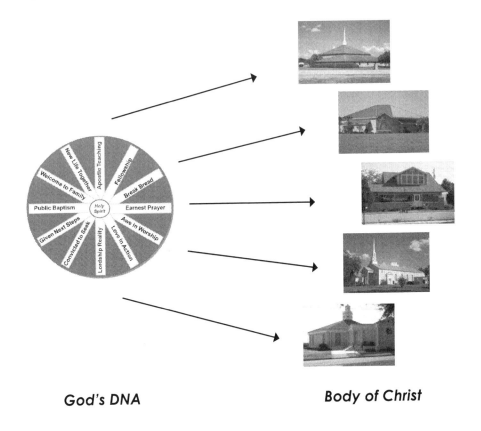

God's DNA   **Body of Christ**

Pray for the Spirit's work in us!

Now if you are ready to get going on that Journey with Jesus . . . let's ask for God's grace to grant us the privilege of traveling in Him,

"Father, for too long I have tried to make things happen in my life as a believer. I have genuinely wanted you to work in my life but I have always been taught that it somehow depended on me. And as I looked at my life, I only saw failure. But it's your presence that I need not some program.

I never really understood that it is your presence in my life that enables me to do what you want me to do. And since

you are in control of my life, it's "OK" for you to set the pace of that work being achieved! Help me keep in step with your Spirit as I abide in Christ and Christ abides in me.

Please help me trust you for what you have promised to do in my life! You are the one who has called me and anointed my life with your Holy Spirit. You have given him to me as a seal of your promise to complete your work in me and fulfill all the good promises you have for me in Christ. And if that were not enough, your very presence reminds me that I am yours and nothing can change that. Your power is sufficient to deal with whatever I face so that you fulfill your life plan for me. So why should I be afraid of anything?

I can't wait to see what your DNA does in my life! I can't wait to see who I am becoming because you are transforming me into the image of Jesus! Help me encourage others on their journeys so that they might discover the joy of knowing just how awesome you are!

There are lots of things that I will never know, but I do know that you have a grand purpose for my life; one that you are fashioning me for right now as your Holy Spirit works in me. Oh, Lord, thank you that I am beginning to see what you are doing in my life.

It is just what Paul prayed when he prayed for the believers in Corinth, "I also pray that the eyes of your heart may be enlightened in order that you may know the hope to which he has called you, the riches of his glorious inheritance in the saints, and his incomparable great power for us who believe. That power is like the working of his mighty strength, which he exerted in Christ when he raised him from the dead and seated him at his right hand in the heavenly realms, far above all rule and authority, power and dominion, and every title that can be given, not only in the present age but also in the age to come. And God placed all things under his feet and appointed him to be head over everything for the church, which is his body, the fullness of him who fills everything in every way" (Ephesians 1:18-22).

And so I join my brethren in crying out, "Father . . . We're ready now . . . We sense your Spirit's presence in our lives . . . We're not afraid any more. Jesus really is on the Throne ruling the universe so that we will be blessed . . . so that your Body will be blessed. You have filled us with Your Spirit to transform us individually and coorporately. Nothing can separate us from your love . . . or make us fearful of letting our lives go into your hands . . . So lead us on our journey in Jesus . . . that others might not be afraid . . . . They also need to hear of who you are . . . and what you are doing!"

This paradigm is offered in the hopes that you will see how the spiritually genetic traits discussed in this book can combine to transform anyone's life. God's DNA is at work in all believers and the more we seek him the more the Body of Christ will see his Spirit's work. May he continue to work in us!

Journey in Jesus

As God's sons and daughters we are being transformed by His Spirit into the image of His Son!

(Jn. 3:7; 14:20; Rm. 8:15-17; 2 Cor. 1:21-22; Acts 2:33; Col. 1:27; 1 Thes. 1:4-10)

DNA of Spiritual Cell

Christ has poured
Out His Spirit...

Acts 2:33

...bringing to us
His Life in power

Acts 1:8

The Adventure is Created by God's DNA in Us!

A Portrait of the Holy Spirit's Transforming Ministry!

(Lk. 3:16; Acts 2:22-47; 2 Cor. 3:3,16-18; 5:17; Gal. 5:25)

1. Lordship Reality........Christ is now enthroned as Lord of glory– Acts 2:29-36
2. Conviction.................We are driven to faith in Christ– Gal. 3:22-24; 1 Thes. 1:5
3. Given Next Steps.......Practical direction for following–Lk. 3:10-14; Acts 2:37-38
4. Public Baptism..........Reflects New Life beginning–Mt.28:19; Acts 2:41; Rm. 6:4
5. Welcome to Family... God's Welcome comes through us– Lk. 14:23; Act 10:47
6. New Life Together.....We are not called to journey alone– Acts 2:41-42; 4:32-35
7. Apostle's Teaching... Grow in their knowledge/faith– 1 Pt. 2:2; 2 Tim. 3:14-17
8. Fellowship............... Called to "one another life"– Jn. 13:14, 34; Rm. 15:7
9. Break Bread............ Committed to the journey until He comes–1 Cor 11:26
10. Earnest Prayer......... God's Kingdom to come– Mt. 6:10; 7:7; Acts 4:31; 12:5
11. Awe in Worship.........Christ is exalted in obvious ways–Rm. 12:1; 1 Cor. 14:25
12. Love in Action.......... Dangerous love meeting real needs–Lk. 10:33; Heb. 13:2

Don Broadwater
Blueprint for Ministry
www.journeyinjesus.com

Made in the USA
Lexington, KY
26 December 2009